Being of Earth

Stella Longland

a Cave of Clay book

Copyright © Stella Longland 2018

Cover design by Stella Longland ©

second edition 2018
with text revisions

All rights reserved. No part of this publication may be reproduced, stored in a retrieval system, or transmitted in any form or by any means without prior written permission of the copyright owner. Nor can it be circulated in any form of binding or cover other than that in which it is published and without similar condition including this condition being imposed on a subsequent purchaser.

(first edition 2016 copyright © Stella Longland 2016)

British Library Cataloguing in Publication Data
A catalogue record for this book is available from the British Library

ISBN 978-1-9999024-3-8

I
eye
ah - ii
purity meets awareness

in carrying

This story was written by from the texts of audio tapes recorded in a state of consciousness somewhere between the worlds out there and the world of everyday.

I thank the Power that brought these experiences to me.

<u>Consult the final 7 pages to find</u>
About the Ancestors
About Language
About Guidance
About the Medicine Wheel
Other Books by the Author
Images index
Contents index

contents

Summer .... Dream of a Running Buffalo
Autumn .... The Cage
Winter .... The Constant   Washing   Utterly Consumed
Spring .... The Strength of the Buffalo

Summer .... Sun Moon Dance   Killing the Bison   Walking with Intent
Autumn .... Entering the Cave   The Work at Hand
Winter Solstice .... The Gift Arrives   The Lights   The Spirit House of the Buffalo
.... A Sacred Knot   The Blue Buffalo
New Year .... The Long Road   The Black Buffalo   In the Spirit Lodge
Spring .... In the Peace Chamber   Through the Spirit Lodge
.... The Healing Guide   In Deep Water   In Deep Earth
.... The Silver Streams   Dream of Running Buffalo
.... Where to Teeter?   Moving North

Summer .... The Necessity of Falling   Calling   Supporting the World
.... The Exam   The Power and I
Autumn .... The Consciousness of the Lodge
Winter .... Give Up the Drug   The Fire Ceremony
.... Dark Waters   Entering the Black Buffalo
Spring .... The Fall

Summer .... The Mycelium   Draw On the Abundance
.... The Silver Cords   The Ancient Ones
Autumn .... A Song to the Buffalo
Winter .... Out Of Darkness Came Light   The Abundance of Our Planet
A New Beginning ... The Gift of the Green

This is a diagram of the 8 energy centres of the travelling body expressed here in the colours of day and night, demonstrating harmonious duality.

As I entered meditation, I heard:

"Your body is the temple of your spiritual life."

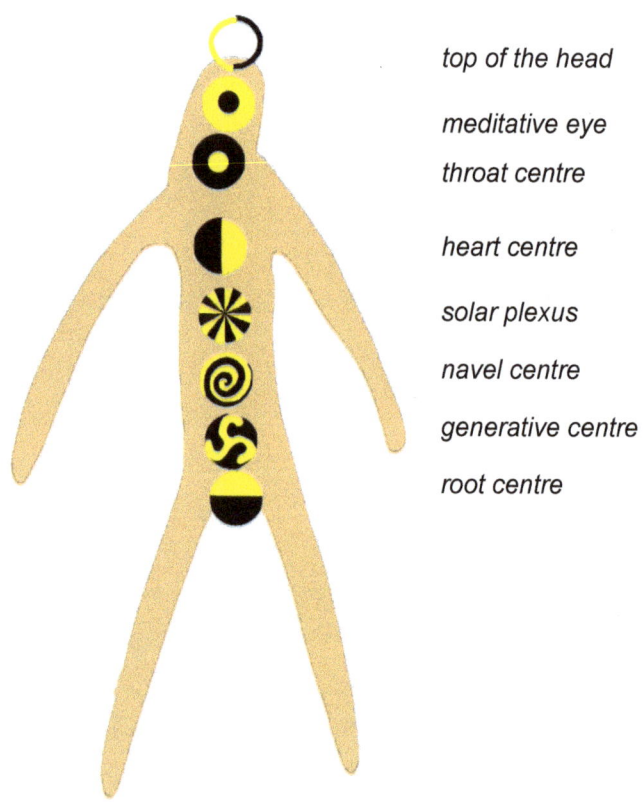

top of the head

meditative eye

throat centre

heart centre

solar plexus

navel centre

generative centre

root centre

Summer

Dream of a Running Buffalo

This morning I woke up dreaming about a Buffalo. In the dream the healing group that I am a member of were meeting in a house. There was a herd of buffalo browsing outside, but one, a young bull, had somehow got into the house. He was on the rampage, full of energy, running loose. I was shocked by his power, appalled, because if he decided to attack we would be instantly dead, but the energy of his presence, the noise of his breathing and his running were awesome.

Hoping to avoid his attention, we flattened ourselves against the walls and he thundered past us out through the open door of the room. We quickly shut that door to trap him in the corridor. Looking through the glass panel in the door, I watched him run to the end of the passage. His way blocked he spun round and headed back, smashing straight through the door as if it were paper. There was unstoppable power in that brown bull. Somebody was coming who knew what had to be done.

Autumn

The Cage

My daily practise of trance travelling started with the colour white completely overcoming me. Well taught to journey in the worlds beyond in the company of a power animal, I thought: "If I can find the Coyote I will follow him, if I can connect with him." I did connect. He began to travel downwards; I followed.

We came to the heart where the colours today were green and purple and the Coyote walked on down. I followed him to a barrier, which was composed of black and yellow spokes, and we went through into the solar plexus world below. This world was illuminated by the palest yellow light and the ground was silvery grey but we did not stop there.

We went on, down into the colour red, the generative centre, very abstract; there was a red spot and then there was a green spot, like traffic lights: stop, go, stop, go, stop, go. He said: "Do you want to stop here?" and I said: "No."

He went on down into the root centre. I followed him but I had difficulty focusing on what was there because, although it was pitch dark, I could see a multitude of shiny, reflected, refracted colours. They reminded me of the shimmering colours you see in coal: glittering purples, iridescent greens, metallic blues. I didn't seem to be able to enter fully into that place today and I was struggling.

We retraced our steps and, when we reached the solar plexus again, I sat down on the muddy silver ground to bathe in the pale gold light. I looked around and I saw my backbone and the cage of my ribs. They were like bars on a window that I was looking through and beyond them stretched a great plain. I sighed: "Oh, it's empty again!" But soon an immense herd of slow-moving buffalo came into view. They wandered along until one was grazing close to the cage of my ribs, the side of its brown head filling my view, the eye level with mine. I gazed into that eye.

Unaccountably the image of a White Buffalo came into my mind. I snorted: "Don't be pretentious!" But no, the whiteness had come. My Teacher had talked two or three times about the White Buffalo, and what did he say? He said: "The appearance of a White Buffalo signifies great changes and a new beginning." I wanted to be part of greatness and newness surely there was a White Buffalo on the plain somewhere. I stood within my wonderful safe cage looking out and I didn't know what to do next.

Winter

The Constant

After connecting with the way that things are internally I noticed there were changes and the Coyote said: "The past has been illuminated. The past will speak." Our attention moved to the centre and my body opened from the centre of seeing down to the root, a bit like if you had split a pea pod and could see the peas, a bit like that. Over to the left the future was dark. Colours began to play on the edge of that darkness, shimmering and moving like the aurora borealis, pinks and blues and greens.

Feeling a little lazy, I thought: "The Coyote can see into the future so I don't need to." As a result of this idle thought, he immediately gave me an opportunity to see ahead. I looked way ahead and I saw a White Buffalo walking towards me. Why of everything I should see that I don't know. At first, the eyes were red, then they were black, then they were yellow, and then they were white. I took one eye and put it in my heart, I took the other eye and put it in my centre of seeing, and a voice said: "When you have completely consumed the buffalo I will still be here."

That was the Coyote speaking, and he gave me the understanding that because I was courageous and could travel on my own and could be on my own and explore on my own and because I loved him without requiring him, he was a constant in my life that would now never leave. "Thank you, Coyote." And he says: "It's down to your own character that this is the case. Your experience and your whole soul life, so you can thank me, but it is part of your Being that this is the case." Then brown-ness came within and that was the Buffalo, the losing of the self, not outside the safe cage of my ribs this time.

Washing

I don't feel too brilliant, there was a heavy frost last night and my body aches. During the night, a spiritual presence came and was still here when I came to get up. I came to meditate and I felt very quiet and connected with that presence.

I was on a wide, open plain, the field of view was vast, and to help myself concentrate deeply I looked down at the ground. There I saw little green shoots. I bent down and leaned close to see them more clearly. Through my feet, I could feel the earth vibrating and I could hear a rumbling sound; a herd of buffalo were coming, I moved quickly to the safety of a mound of large grey boulders.

The buffalo swept into view, a surging torrent, and in among them a White Buffalo ran, coming close to me, washing over me, covering me until I was completely white. I was wondering what it could mean because I didn't have any idea; I remembered that the White Buffalo signifies a time of change, and I remembered the Coyote saying: "When you have completely consumed the buffalo I will still be here."

My attention wandered, I drifted, and when I came back I panicked and called out loudly: "Coyote, I am lost, help me!" and he did help me, he took me back to the memory I had lost, which was the washing with whiteness I have just spoken of, and I experienced it again. Then we travelled down deep, deep down, deep into my lost-ness, deep into the darkness, and I spoke out, saying: "I don't know what I am doing, I am no use whatsoever," and various other statements about myself that seemed to be true.

When I eventually stopped talking, I remembered that I had

recently discovered the colours of my psyche in a meditation, and how could I claim to be lost when I had found them? I decided to go deeper, deeper down, to find them again.

I went down into slime and mud; it was like travelling to the bottom of a pond. I picked up the green and the black colours that were part of me and brought them out of the murkiness. They were all covered with mud and slime and I exclaimed: "Why, mud and slime are almost the colours of these colours!" but they were in a messy state and I realized: "I must wash them in clean water."

"Coyote, help me, I am lost!" and he took me to the limestone moorland of the local Fell, to a dry waterfall there. Only rarely, after exceptional rain, does floodwater cascade over the rim and fall into the stone bowl twenty feet below, a bowl carved in the soft limestone by the power of ancient water and the constant tumbling of water-borne rocks.

Holding the muddied colours in my hands, I knelt down and listened, some way below the dry bed was a hollow space where the river now ran, the river that had carved the bowl. There was not one drop of water to be heard or found and I supposed: "I had better just wait here for some water to come." But the Coyote wasn't for waiting; a torrent of water cascaded over the fall thoroughly drenching me and I declared: "Now, this is washing!" and it was like the beginning of something new.

Soaked through, holding the dripping colours in my hands, I looked up in expectation of another cascade. I looked up the sheer rock walls to the rim of the bowl, thirty feet above me, where luxuriant trees in full leaf added deep shade to the hollow I was in, and I thought: "If those trees were all chopped down there would be more light in this place." I was shocked: "What am I thinking? I love the trees!" but standing among the grey boulders trying to feel that love, I drifted again.

I drifted again and I came to the still, picture-less place which is at the centre of my consciousness and I called again: "Coyote, Coyote, I'm lost, help me!" and he helped me again and gave me back the pictures that I have just spoken of. Without the Coyote, I lost the memories and that meant I was lost, but, if I could just remember to ask him, he would guide me through.

Now that I had all the memories again, I dressed my psyche, my circular psyche, my medicine wheel psyche, in the freshly washed colours, the black to my left (I am looking out of the page at you), the green to my right, with yellow below and blue above.

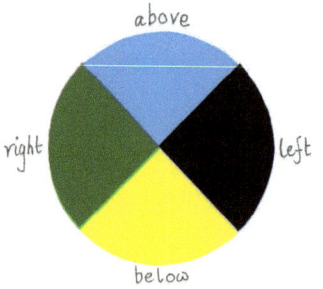

a personal colour wheel

I felt, well, nothing really mind-blowing, I felt, um, ... that I was those four colours and I felt free of conflict.

Utterly Consumed

As I meditated before sleeping, a landscape opened up that was very powerful and strange to me but I had not got it in me to stay there. I did see bison and, when I looked at them closely, I noticed that they were very like trees. It came to me that we had consumed the bison. When there had been millions and millions of them, it looked as if they could never diminish. Suddenly the millions were gone. This was repeating now with the trees. Yes, those photographs from the nineteenth century of the piles of buffalo skulls from the slaughters are like the pictures of log piles at a present day logging company site.

Spring

The Strength of the Buffalo

I picked up the Roe Deer skull; a gift I was given by the spirits when I broke through some of my inhibitions. I will always know that it was through my own effort that I received this gift. I often meditate with it and today I lay down and placed it on my body at the level of my heart.

Last night, as darkness came, the sky was a deep luminous blue and this reminded me that the spirit world is ever-present. As I lay meditating, I was trying to make sense of what my purpose is and that deep blue colour changed to the palest gold. In the gold, a voice asked me what I thought I was doing and I said I was trying to express the spirit world in a way that would be evident to other people so that they could connect to it: nothing fancy, just something on an individual level.

I had answered the question and I found myself standing upright. I looked down and the ground wasn't green, wasn't grass, it was brown. It was bare beaten earth and one single Buffalo, the same colour as the earth, was standing there. This Buffalo was massive and I tried to connect my energy centres to him. In attempting to do this, it came to my understanding that, unlike me, he had no self-will in his solar plexus, but, when it came to the heart, the heart of the Buffalo was bold and strong and I connected to that heart, I needed that strength. When that was done he fell on his knees and was absorbed into the earth.

I looked around and I noticed a familiar mound of large grey boulders; it was the place of safety, where the White Buffalo had washed me with the colour white. I noticed that where the grey stones touched the brown earth there were some green shoots of grass, just a handful, not more than a dozen probably. They were vibrant with energy, but so few! I tipped my body over to look closer. The skull of the Deer was on my chest and water poured from the horns of the Deer onto this grass to help it grow.

Summer

Sun Moon Dance

In July, my Teacher left for America to take part in a ceremony. While he was there, he learned that the first Sun Moon Dance in the UK was soon to take place in Manchester, only an hour from where I lived. He rang me to let me know. It was ten days away and I knew I would go. When I told my partner that the Dance entailed not eating or drinking for three to four days he was furiously upset and shouted: "But you don't even know these people; you could die!" Nevertheless, I knew I would dance.

Nine days have passed and I am going to Manchester this afternoon to meet up with the people organising the ceremony and, in a day's time, I will participate in my first Sun Moon Dance. I have had to witness some of my weaker points during the last few days. One of the most extreme was yesterday afternoon when I found myself saying to myself: "Why am I doing this? I don't even like people! I have never done anything for anybody; it is not in my nature, so why am I going to participate in a ceremony to help the People?" I am just hoping all the fear and self-dissuasion will diminish as I get into the process of the Dance. The weather yesterday was dreadful with a ripping wind; it seemed appropriate and might help to blow all my rubbish away.

When I meditated my centre of seeing was open and the colour white filled it. The colour black filled my heart. The colour black in my heart was not bad, it was the Great Mystery, and I needed to learn something about my heart. I went into my heart to find my greater self and I thought this might be what I would do during the Dance this coming weekend. I saw a blue crystal in there. I understood that when my heart is open my throat will also open and I will be able to speak about my experiences. But my body is not so brilliant; I feel bloated and uncomfortable, a bit sluggish and verging on fat. What a lovely description!

I got to Manchester just after three in the afternoon, found the flat I was looking for, and then, because I was early, I walked down the street and had a coffee. When I came back and met one of the organisers, I was asked to sign a consent form that began with: 'I understand fully the nature of the Dances', so, jokingly, I crossed that out and put instead: 'I do not fully understand' and I signed it.

In the evening, we went to a local hall to hear the Chief and his daughter, the drum chief, talk about the Dance and the work. They were close relations of Joseph Rael, Beautiful Painted Arrow, Teacher of Mysteries, who was given the Sun Moon Dance in vision with the instruction that it was for all peoples. Now, it was being given to us. I got my first look at Joseph's brother; I liked him, he was solid, straightforward, unpretentious.

At the end of the meeting, he told us all to be on site at nine a.m. as there was a lot to do. Someone, who was acting as his chauffeur, told me there was no chance they would be there by then but I decided to get there at that time anyway; might as well start by trying to follow the suggestions of the Chief.

The next morning, Friday, I left Manchester early and eventually found the Dance site, which was located in the Cheshire countryside about forty minutes from the city. On a large hay field that had recently been cut, the circular arbour, the dance ground delineated by wooden posts, was half built and there were also two tipis spaced well apart. I decided to walk around before introducing myself. On the far side of the field, a steep incline led down to a small stream the banks of which were a mass of willow trees mixed with other trees such as oaks and ashes. It was very pleasant to have the trees so close.

I walked on to the tipi where there seemed to be the most activity. Someone handed me a cup of tea and I sat down with the others on the ground in front of the tipi. Admiring the fresh white canvas, I noticed a skull hanging above the door flap. There was no doubt that it was a Buffalo skull, a very beautiful one.

After chatting for a while, getting to know the people, I wandered off for a quiet moment. When I came back, I passed the door of the second tipi, which was nearer to the arbour. Looking in through the open door flap, I saw that the Buffalo skull had been moved, and was now lying, with flower offerings around it, on a blanket inside. Not realizing that someone was in there, I went in and saw the keeper of the skull standing there. We did not speak, but, as he left, he smudged me with sage, and I sat down alone.

I sat and looked at the skull, a deep and terrible sadness came over me. Similar to the sadness that comes to me with a persistent 'memory' that everyone I love is missing; that I had been away, and when I came back; they were gone. In this 'memory' there is a fear that maybe I did something wrong. I don't seek to understand it; I recognise it as a trigger that motivates me now. In the tipi the feeling that everything I cherished was gone, utterly gone and totally destroyed, came back to me. The loss of the buffalo herds summed up this loss. I cried and cried. Great love was pouring from the spirit of the Buffalo towards me and this intensified my feelings.

I came out of there completely different, vulnerable and ready to cry at anything. This especially manifested itself over the subject of tents. The information sheet that had been sent to me specifically said there was no need for dancers to bring a tent. Now I was here I clearly needed a tent. I needed somewhere to store my stuff and somewhere to sleep if I left the Dance early, somewhere to change for the sweat lodge and somewhere to change after the Dance was over. I felt utterly miserable that I had not brought my tent and deeply let down by the people who sent the instructions. Why, on the one occasion that I did what I was told had it all gone horribly wrong? I was overcome with self-pity and recrimination. I felt an unaccustomed anguish at being let down, so odd, because I think I am so used to being let down.

At the same time as I was devastated the strength of my feelings struck me as ludicrous particularly as I had been buoyant and happy before I went into the medicine tent. That is what the second tipi was, the medicine tent.

I had got over all this by the time the Chief arrived. I met him and his daughter walking down the field towards the bank where the trees grew. He was carrying a chain saw. I made some disparaging remark about using a chain saw to cut down the Dance Tree. His daughter countered by saying that we had to accept that modern technology was part of our lives and how did I get to the ceremony. I replied: "I came in my fourth body, my car!" and we all laughed. The Tree had already been chosen. We prepared to cut it. The Chief announced that we were going to cut it down with an axe, and this is what we did.

We, the dancers, carried the Tree back up to the field. I say 'we', but I was too short and really didn't carry any weight. I was glad about this. I felt none too strong. When the Tree did touch my shoulder, it felt so heavy I seemed to buckle at the knees. We laid it down outside the arbour and everyone helped to prepare it. The lower half was stripped of bark, and all the sharp points removed from this section, the scars were sealed and blackened with charcoal. Most of the branches were cut from the upper section. This left a single trunk that split into two branches about four fifths of the way up, making a Y-shape. Leaf bundles were prepared and tied to the arms of the Y. The Buffalo skull was brought out of the medicine tipi and tied onto the Tree at the fork. An Eagle feather was hung on each horn.

Tobacco offerings wrapped in long strips of cloth, one for each of the four medicine wheel colours, were tied to the tops of the two arms of the Y, looking at the Tree from outside the east gate of the arbour, the black and white to the left, the red and yellow to the right. Another set of coloured cotton strips were tied round the point where the stripped trunk met the bark, in ascending order: yellow, white, black, and red. When all was ready, we carried the Tree into the arbour, raised and slid it into the hole with the aid of steadying ropes; it went in perfectly. The hole was slowly filled with loose soil tamped down until the Tree stood firm.

Now the dancers should choose their places and bring what they needed into the arbour. I chose the space next to where the drum would be, next to the east gate. I brought my sleeping bag, mat and a few other things to my place and put on my sweat lodge shift. The fire, heating the lodge stones, had been burning for some hours and now we went into the lodge. It was dusk. After the sweat, a drink of water was offered and slices of watermelon were passed around, the melon tasted exquisitely delicious. This was our last food and drink.

It was time to enter the arbour and we went to our places. The Chief addressed us all and told us that whatever we had done, whether we knew what it was or not, we should forgive ourselves. I knew I was going to have trouble with this. Sure enough, during the first night I wrestled with the concept of forgiveness. I found that I could not forgive myself. I couldn't just say to myself: "I forgive you." It was not enough. I had to do something, rectify something. I knew that my greater self had no lack of forgiveness, in fact, it did not judge, but I could not grant myself forgiveness here, my small self could not forgive myself. At some point, I came to terms with the fact that I could not follow the Chief's instruction on this. I was not into forgiveness; I was into doing something to set matters straight.

When I began to get ill, I did wonder if my inability to forgive myself catapulted me into sickness. But before the pain started I was already quite fearful about my energy levels and I had another fear as well, which was about possession, a fear that the spiritual energy was going to come and grab me, extinguish my free will, and somehow I would be lost.

Maybe in the second dance of Saturday morning, a communication came through the Tree. It said: "You come of your own free will. There is no compulsion here. If you are called, it is your choice to come to the Tree." Hearing that made me feel much better, after that I felt that if the opportunity came, and it wasn't absolutely sure that the Tree would call me, but if it did, I had the choice as to whether I went or not and that made a huge difference to me at that moment. Now I could dance and not be held back by fear.

Then the journey started. I didn't understand it at the time, but now it seems to me to have been a rapid journey through all the surrounding levels of the astral plains into the clearer spiritual worlds, and that it was necessary so that I could find purity in order to hear spiritually while being completely conscious in this world of the Earth. It was a purifying of my body, so that on Sunday I could dance truly for the good of all. That seems to me to be what Saturday was about, because most of that day I was semi-conscious, especially in the times between the dance rounds.

I don't remember how the illness started, but I found my solar plexus to be knotting up and a headache to be hovering. Sometime in the morning, at the end of a dance round, I was very violently sick. The energy rush came from very low down, below my diaphragm, and the spew was white foam, nothing but white foam. Oh, the last thing I needed was to lose fluid like this! I tried to lie on my back and meditate but this caused severe pain in my solar plexus so I lay in a heap and experienced some strange things. At the end of the following two dances, I threw up again. In among all this there were at least three experiences of travelling at speed along a road in a car being driven by another person. The car was going so fast, it was making me sick; the blurred landscape flashing by and the swerving motion of the car were making me sick.

The headache became more and more terrible and there was a constant involvement on the astral plain. Conversations with people I had never seen before, pointless and inane, involvement in processes belonging to the spirits there that had nothing to do with me. I could clearly recognise this at the time but I could do nothing about it.

The spirits kept bringing me drinks and food. I saw jugs of water and plates of delicious food clearly and often during the afternoon. I don't remember drinking or eating them, but, contrary to what I thought would happen, I became neither thirsty nor hungry. Among all this, I would hear snatches of the Dance songs and I hung onto them for dear life.

Then there was the possibility that I had heat stroke. The symptoms I was having were very similar to the symptoms I had in Italy when I threw up in the cave of the Sibyl at Cumae. I remembered how my partner looked after me, booked us into a hotel, dunked me under a cold shower, and then sat by me all night while I slept it off. What I was experiencing physically now was so similar it brought back how caring he had been of me then.

There were some attendants in the arbour called Moon Mothers but I didn't understand their role and, because I got up to dance each round and threw up in the rest periods, they didn't yet know I was in trouble and I thought: "Nobody is caring for me now. Maybe I will get delirious." Then I thought: "But these guys are all from a hot country and they must know the symptoms of heat stroke and they will not let me get that sick. Oh well, if I die, I die." I was feeling rather dramatic, but it was also dawning on me that this sickness had spirit visions with it and seemed to be part of a process and that made it different to the italian illness. And, how could I get severe heat stroke in two hours on a slightly warmer than average but hardly hot english summer day?

In the middle of all that terrible turmoil, I was seriously wondering if I would be able to stay in the Dance. I saw clearly that I would not be able to tolerate the rest of my life if I didn't make it through and yet it seemed that my body was conking out. In the depths of this battle I heard a quiet voice that was my Teacher, Alexander, and, behind him, his Teacher, Joseph, and beyond them another voice, like echoes of each other. I heard two words spoken in a serious and encouraging tone: "Come on!"

The Chief walked past and I told him I was being sick. He said: "That happens sometimes." I nodded: "Oh, I thought it was probably ok." He sent one of the Moon Mothers to me. I lay with my head in her lap and she soothed me. She suggested that the headache might be caffeine toxin. I wondered how she knew I drank too much coffee, especially the day before. I thanked her for looking after me and I called her: "Mother." To my surprise, I found this very easy and I remembered what a mother was.

That night I slept deeply. I woke early and saw the Tree in the pre-dawn light. It looked so wonderful, numinous and charged with energy that it made a deep impression on me. When we got up to sing to the sunrise, I felt I might be better. The Chief came and asked me how I was. "Better, I think, better." I danced all day and my energy rose and rose and rose. I found myself now able to dance with intent.

This began early in the morning. The trees all poked their heads over the top of the arbour and called to me. In reply I danced to create the meditation vision I had a few months ago where a tree was a fountain from which issued the four colours of the medicine wheel in the form of branches. Below the ground, the brown roots made a reverse fountain that dived down and then returned to the surface. The branches descended and the roots rose and they met at ground level to form a sort of dynamo.

To achieve the vision of the coloured fountain made by the branches I danced the colour of each direction and visualized an environment from that direction that typified the colour. I began with the West and danced Black: I danced the plains of America black with buffalo. In the South, I danced White and visualized the Antarctic. In the East, I danced Yellow and visualized the Sahara desert. I hoped my geography was correct. In the North, I danced Red and danced for the lava fields and volcanoes of Iceland. The local trees crowded in and the colour green spread everywhere.

As I danced the fountains above and felt the trees draw near, I saw that the palms of my hands were glowing with the colour green. Circles of green filled the centres of my palms; they were not spheres lying on my hands but circles of energy in the palms of my hands and this was healing energy. I danced my palms, drew energy from the Tree into them, and sent it out again to the world.

It may have been then that the european Buzzard soared above and came to be visible in the Y of the Tree, and in the rest period between this and the next dance I felt the Buffalo enter me from the root up. It rose until it filled me to my heart. The skull of the Buffalo, the dead Buffalo, the self-sacrificing Buffalo, came to rest in my heart. Then the Eagle came round my head and into my head and was my head. I understood that it was given to me that I could dance the next dance in honour of the Buffalo and the Eagle. I did that. I danced the Buffalo to a certain point towards the Tree, and then I danced the Eagle from there on in. This turned out to be the last dance of the day. As I danced, I heard this: "Till the End of Time." I understood that this kind of spiritual Dance and interchange between incarnate and discarnate Beings would continue until the end of time and also that I would be there too, dancing.

Photographs are not taken during ceremony but before and after that's ok. I took a few while we were setting up and also at the end before we took the arbour down. Returning home I got them developed and looking through them before my partner came in I decided that I would not show him the pictures of the Dance Tree. This was partly a desire to keep it secret and partly cowardice on my part because I knew him very well and I knew that those photos would be perfect for him to launch an attack on my spiritual quest. There was one photo of the arbour from a distance and poking up above the blue tarpaulins and the surrounding trees was the top of the Dance Tree. I left that photo in the pile saying to myself: "If he notices the Tree there then I will show him the others." Well, he did notice it and when I showed the rest, he looked at them quietly and carefully and made no remarks at all.

the tree above the arbour

It was not long after the Sun Moon Dance that my partner went to America for a holiday. When he returned, he told me some interesting stories about encounters that he had while he was there, in particular his meeting with an old man sitting under a tree, and he told me that there was a gift coming from America for me. It was all rather mysterious and I decided to try to forget about it until the gift arrived.

Killing the Bison

As soon as I woke up, I was aware of the presence of the Chief. When I came to meditate, I was calm and still and he was there. I heard the Coyote say: "The Chief is going to give you the gift he gave you at the Sun Moon Dance." A process occurred in which I was tied to the Tree at the level of my solar plexus with the four colours of the medicine wheel. My head was where the Buffalo skull hung and I experienced sneaking up on the browsing herd, no horses, sneaking up on them and stabbing them in the neck, the red blood pouring out and covering us, the hunters. The animal trying to get up, shuddering and dropping dead and we would lie there with our dead bison. The herd being unaware of the cause of these deaths moved on, and we skinned and used every part of those we had killed.

I don't know if this ever happened, but it is a metaphor of taking what you need without disturbing everything else. Yes, there was something very ok about that way of killing; it was sacrificial, dangerous, took us to the limits of our skill and safety, and kept us alive.

Walking with Intent

A month later, attending a seminar led by my Teacher, I took a drum journey. I felt myself lifting; I was being lifted up by an Eagle who carried me, like a piece of carrion, up the course of the dry river bed. My body was hanging limply in the Eagle's talons and, dangling there, I pondered my fate.

I assumed: "I am dead." Then I thought: "No, I am not dead because I am still conscious." .... "Oh, the Eagle is going to drop me from a great height onto the rocks to break all the bones in my body to make me easier to eat." The Eagle didn't do that. I thought another thought: "The Eagle is going to fly to the eyrie and feed me to the Eaglets." But the Eagle didn't do that.

The Eagle flew for a long, long time, until he eventually landed on a cliff ledge. I saw a vertical golden crack in the rock face; the Eagle pushed me into this crack with his beak. I got the feeling that the golden crack was an opening in the breast of the very Eagle that had carried me. I went through that crack; it was the entrance into the heart centre of the Eagle.

Within the crack, I met the two Coyotes. I took their hands in joy and relief and said with surprise: "I've found you here!" One was Black and one was Yellow, and something, which I can't quite remember now, was the colour White. Only the colour Red was needed to complete the medicine wheel, so I determined to supply the colour Red by becoming it.

The Red was at the bottom and the White was at the top, the Black Coyote was to the right and the Yellow Coyote was to the left. It was not the medicine wheel as Joseph teaches it, Joseph, Teacher of mysteries, Alexander's Teacher and through Alexander, my Teacher. The wheel needed to be turned so that the Red was at the top in the North, Yellow in the East, White in the South and Black in the West. I couldn't work out exactly how to make it right, so I just let it happen and, by various means of twisting and turning, it was achieved. There was the medicine wheel as Joseph teaches it.

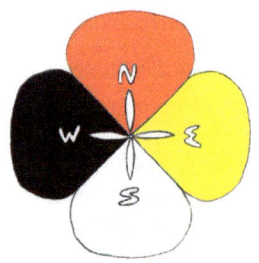

colours of the directions

The wheel began to spin. Then it fractured. I saw the Black, the Yellow, and the Red fly away like jagged lightning flashes. I was left alone with the colour White. I stood in the white space waiting.

A young woman approached me who was dressed all in white. She came close, then turned and began to walk away. I followed her. As we walked, I asked her a question: "How can I walk straight?" I asked this because earlier in the day I couldn't walk straight. The seminar group took a meditative walk to the beach to understand the art of walking and, when we arrived, we sought a blessing from the ocean. As I walked towards the sea, I was staggering all over the place. That is why I asked the woman: "Teach me to walk in a straight line."

She danced a very strange dance; a shuffling dance, where the steps seemed to move backwards while she went forwards. Her head was down, her body leaned slightly forward, her arms were held straight but pointing to the ground behind her. It was a concentrate-on-the-ground dance. Step forward with the right foot to touch the ground with the toes, then pull the foot backwards and place it halfway along the left foot so that the heel of the right foot rests in the instep of the left foot. Take a similar step with the left foot. Then repeat this step with the right foot, but instead of putting weight on it as it rests on the ground by the instep of the left foot, drag it back farther along the ground so that both feet are level. Pause and stand for one moment, and then step forward with the left foot and, leading with this step by the left foot, start the sequence again. That is the dance she taught me, a pawing-the-ground dance.

When the drumming changed, I came back. Later in the day, I remembered how the medicine wheel colours worked. It was like this: I went forward with the Coyotes on either side, the Black and the Yellow. Ahead was White, into which we walked, and in there was the White Buffalo. I saw the White Buffalo in the space inside the Eagle and that is how the colour White came into the medicine wheel. Then the only colour that was left to find was the Red and, to complete the medicine wheel, I took on that colour at that time. So the mystery about who supplied the form for the colour white is solved.

Autumn

Entering the Cave

Last night I went to visit my friend from the healing group and we spent the evening together. At the end of the evening, we meditated. A strange black two-dimensional creature, like a paper cutout, came to me and, beckoning me to follow, led me through a dark entrance. It was a very weird creature and I decided not to try to consider what it was.

Seeking an alternative area of study, I noticed that the walls and floors of the tunnel we entered were studded with tiny crystal points and I saw the colours green and purple and blue and yellow shining there. I rolled my body on these points. I think this made the black shape a little impatient but it was so physically delightful for me that I rolled and rolled on them and felt them prickling all my body, as if my spirit body was coming alive. I thought of explaining this to the incomprehensible black Being but I gave up the idea as impossible.

We travelled on. The deeper we went, the narrower the tunnel became. An earthworm, a golden earthworm, which emitted its own light, came and led the way. We went on, down through the wormholes, until we entered a vast underground chamber that was only accessible via the tubes made by worms. In the chamber, a beautiful soft light was apparent and I assumed that we must have entered a gold mine or, perhaps, a treasure cave of the deep earth Beings.

I noticed a Gnome sitting there, surprisingly, to me, wearing a jacket and trousers. He was short in stature but not ugly and not unfriendly, so I asked him: "What makes the earth-light?" He said: "What do you think it is?" I tried to decide whether it came from the crystal jewels, or, if not, how else it could be generated. I couldn't find the answer. I repeated my question and he said: "Come and sit next to me." I sat down beside him and he continued: "If you want to know you must become one with the consciousness of the place." He paused and asked: "Are you afraid?" What he meant was: "Are you afraid of merging your consciousness with mine?"

Then I realized that from the beginning of this journey into the Earth, I had felt extremely confident and safe, and now here I was, without giving it a thought, about to join my consciousness with a deep earth Being that I had never met before. With a quick laugh, I answered: "Probably." I didn't want to sound too cocky and although I felt sure that there must be some fear somewhere in my psyche, I wasn't going to look for it and it wasn't going to stop me.

We sat together, his arm round my shoulder, and I entered the consciousness. After a while I spoke: "Oh, we imagine the light and that is how it comes to be." I said this from his consciousness, and he said: "Yes, that's right, and the world becomes as you imagine it, so if you want it to be beautiful and light and interesting, imagine it so. Or if you want it to be simple and explicable and comprehensible, well, imagine it so!"

The Work at Hand

The meditation started with my seeing rank upon rank of spirits in front of me, and reaching an understanding that these were all spirits who wished to help in the work at hand. They were there in vast numbers. I looked and looked, turning my head to the left and to the right to try to see them all and finally bringing my attention back to the centre where the tall Spirit of the North stood.

Through the Northern Spirit the Buffalo came, red ties were on one horn and blue on the other. I felt the snorting of his breath and the colour green seemed to emanate from his nostrils. I entered the Brown Buffalo; this process took a very, very long time and I can't really say how many changes of state happened there. There were many give-aways and openings and acceptances required on my part in order to be there, all of which I am willing to do, but my lifetime programming occasionally gets in the way.

After entering completely into the psyche of the Buffalo, a hole opened up in front of me and I was overcome by the feeling that I was going to enter the Buffalo's digestive system. This I really did not want to do and yet I knew that if it was the next thing that had to be done I should do it. I saw a shaft leading downwards and I descended. Reaching the bottom, I came into a village. The houses were leather-covered mounds with straight poles at the doors. In the middle of the village was a huge Tree. I went straight to the Tree. I lingered there; I didn't hurry on, I allowed its magnetism to slowly draw me in.

I went into the golden-yellow interior of the Tree and the place I entered contained the Ancient Grandfather, the Grandfather with the long grey hair who is the messenger of love. A little voice said: "I, I, I." That was me hanging on to my ego, and I knew I must stop it. I began to say: "You, you, you," and to appreciate the Grandfather. Although better, this was not quite correct. I chose: "We, we, we."

When I was completely 'we' with the Grandfather, he bent down and began to dig into a bank. He pulled a nature Being out of the ground, a brown, squiggling, screeching Being which was expending its energy to divert my attention. It was a very peculiar sound, it made my mind slip, and the Grandfather said to me very gently: "Concentrate on the nature Being." So I looked at it again. It was still screaming and writhing as if the Grandfather were trying to kill it. He uncurled it, a bit like a hedgehog, and did something to it. Then he let it go, put it back in the ground again.

I began to come back through a lot of things that, huh, have gone! I tried to think afterwards what it was all about and why I was there as an observer and I feel that in that experience is the reason why I am important. I am important because of being incarnated here with independent thought. I don't know whether this is true, or why I should need to be here to be there to see that, but the very deep feeling I had all the way through the experience was that I was sure it was the right thing for me to be doing even though it didn't suit my ego particularly well.

I remember saying at one point: "Goodness, is it really like this?" Something was happening that seemed to my mind very, very peculiar and I just had to stand back and accept it but now it seems that I was unable to carry any memory of it back. As I had entered the body of the Buffalo, I had heard that I was entering a sacred space of complete safety. The deep appreciation of that enabled me to take this journey and also to accept with minimal protest everything that came.

When I returned I felt very good and I saw again all the ranks of spirits and I addressed them: "Yes, it is me. I need all the help I can get from everybody who is interested in this project because I have forgotten everything and I don't know what I am doing." Then I was a bit overwhelmed by the thousands of spirits that were there. How would I cope if they all stepped forward to help me? Something told me this was a pretty stupid thought which related only to the human world. Then I thought there must be some spirits in there who weren't perfectly well motivated and this again was pointed out to be a silly thought.

I felt very confused and I called the Coyotes. They came, Black and Yellow, and formed the heart symbol over my spinning solar plexus. I understood that their action was a way to calm the conflict in the solar plexus feelings because the solar plexus at rest is the heart.

Winter Solstice

The Gift Arrives

Today was my last day of work before Christmas. I was out all day until after dark. My partner was away, working too. When I arrived home, some parcels were waiting in the workshop. One was a very large square box, not the size of box that normally comes to our business. It was unmanageably big so I got the sack barrow and took it into the house.

Then it began to dawn on me that it might be the gift, because I saw 'export packing' on the label. I put my glasses on and read 'export declaration: gift, Buffalo skull'. I felt amazed. It was addressed to my partner, so, of course, I didn't open it but I made a ceremony for its arrival, saying: "Welcome!" I played my drum and sang, played my flute and prayed.

After this ceremony, I decided to walk in the moonlight. I went out into the darkness that was like day and took apples to the horses down by the river behind the house. A red horse with a white blaze took all the apples and wouldn't let the others have any, that made me laugh, a dominant bullying horse. I stroked its nose cautiously then I walked on to the oak tree on the river bank. The face of the full Moon was sometimes obscured by clouds but its light was so brilliant that it came right through them. I stood by the tree listening to the sound of the river and watching the Moon, now shining in a briefly clear and brilliantly light night sky. On the way back, hoping for more apples, the horse greeted me. I passed it by. It walked a few steps with me, then stopped and watched me go.

That night the power of the gift inside the box was such that I had deep spiritual experiences. The next day, while I was out, my partner unpacked it. When I came back he had put it in my study, but I didn't rush to see it. Suddenly I was in no hurry at all. I decided to talk to him first because I wanted to find out as much as I could about where it came from. He told me that the old man he had met in America had visited him recently in dreamtime and spoken to him, but the only instruction he could remember was that I should take the four medicine wheel colours in wool, and plait them through the bottom of the nasal bones, to, as he called it, control the Buffalo. I queried this: "Control? No, I don't think it would be to control." Days later when I came to perform this ceremony I did it with the intention of forming a connection, because that is what came to me. When it was done, I held the plait to each of my energy centres in turn and it welded most strongly to my navel centre like an umbilical cord.

My partner gave the impression that the Buffalo was killed after he visited America in the summer; this coincides with the meditation journey after the Sun Moon Dance when the Chief's gift was shown to me in a vision in which I killed bison. After remembering this, I looked through my meditation documents and I found that the Buffalo had come closer and closer since the Sun Moon Dance in July, and I was awed by the fact that this gift had arrived just as the Moon reached its fullness, which occurred this year on the winter solstice, the shortest, darkest day. It was also the case that the

Moon was closer to the Earth, at this same time, than it had been for hundreds of years. This fact was reported in the newspapers but none of the experts seemed to agree on precisely how many years.

I entered an intense ceremonial space that continued for ten days. On Christmas day, I talked to the Ancient Grandfather. He gave me advice. He told me that my life would be as hard as it had been. He told me it was necessary for me to do some things which might be considered peculiar in our modern life and that I should not allow this to stop the process. I followed his advice.

Things that stick out in my mind are that one night in a state of awakened awareness I was digesting the Buffalo through my solar plexus. I was SO hungry. I was bolting it down like a dog. I couldn't believe how starving I was, I ate the whole animal. I remember thinking at the time with some shock: "How hungry am I?" Another time I came into consciousness with the Buffalo skull hanging in front and just above me. In my inner eye, I could see it there. It stayed visible for ages and I tried to stay with it. If my attention wandered, I could return to the same place and there the skull was, unmoved and unmoving.

The ceremonies that I did over those days just evolved slowly, everything slowly evolved. I allowed myself to be guided and did what inspired me. There was a panic in me somewhere that I didn't know anything but this was so small as to be insignificant. I felt I had gone into a place where everything would unfold without me needing to comprehend it, and it did. The end that was being aimed for need not be thought about because there was to be no such end.

I prayed to the Great Spirit that the Buffalo would teach me. The colour white came to my lower centres, and the colour green opened my eye centre. Then the Brown Buffalo came. I saw something perched between his horns. At first, I felt it was my self, but then I decided to see the otherness of it. I saw a brown nature Being and, at that moment, I understood how I was part of nature and also not part of it. This Being stepped down from between the horns of the Buffalo and came to me and something magical happened between us to do with the earth and the colour brown as a generative force of life on the planet.

The Lights

In the ceremony that came on Christmas day, I gave the Buffalo my heart centre. When I did this, I laid my chest against the bone-white forehead and vast amounts of blue light shot out from the centre of my Being, welding us together in a ball of blue light. When I pulled my body away from this, which I did because it was the time to do it, I fell back breathless and panting from the intensity of the experience. I did not know at the time, but the reason I did pull myself away like that was in order to experience the immense strength of that bonding with the Buffalo by means of the blue light in the heart centre.

When the heart centre ceremony was over, I thought the work was finished and I covered the Buffalo skull up with cloths in order to rest. A certain stage of completion was arrived at then but it wasn't the end. The Power still called me. I felt a surge of love from the Grandfathers and it became clear that there was going to be a solar plexus ceremony. This was difficult. It was so difficult to open my solar plexus. In fact, trying to achieve this took a day of extended stints of four hours at a stretch. I called the Coyotes to help me. They were utterly willing to come and they did help in every way they could. Still I couldn't manage to do what I had done so swiftly in the heart.

After a long struggle, I knew that the time was coming. I knew that the colour green was going to come from my solar plexus, and be given to the Buffalo. But when the process started, the colours went all wrong. Black and yellow, and reds of an unpleasant sort, all seemed to come pouring out in a horrible mess. It was as if some terrible blockages, or poisons, or selfish motivations were the first things to erupt.

Then the colour green did manifest and did enter into the Buffalo and everything was fine and I thought: "Good, when I go to bed tonight the spirits won't shake me like they have been doing." At the beginning of this particular ceremony, I had been shaken. In fact, I remember now, the night the Buffalo was first here, still in the box, the shaking got so bad that the whole of the top of my body came off the bed and I was thrown back down again. My head hit the pillow with a thump.

When this type of thing is going on, I am peculiarly detached. I try not to influence it or do anything about it at all, but just to be an observer, and, yes, after the solar plexus had given up its green light to the Buffalo I thought that the shaking would stop. But it did not, and I thought: "That shows how much I know!" The following morning I was able to make the colour green in my solar plexus and form it into a ball in my hands, which I fed into the mouth of the Buffalo as food.

At the very end of all the work on the solar plexus a beautiful ceremony came. I took four pieces of coloured cloth. I carefully cut them all to the same length with the prayer: "May the colours be balanced in the medicine wheel." Then I took them one by one, starting with the Yellow, then White, then Black, and then Red, and, holding them in turn up towards the Great Spirit, I tied the yellow to the tip of the left horn of the Buffalo. I tied the white to the base of that same horn. Next, I tied the black to the tip and the red to the base of the right horn. As I took each strip of cloth I spoke the name of the colour, the cardinal direction, and the meaning as they are given in Joseph's teachings, then I took an in-breath and sang their sound. On each note, as I ran out of breath, I pulled the knot tight.

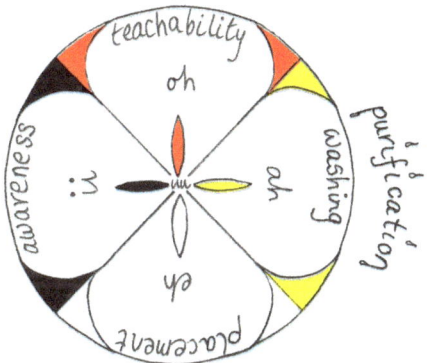

more about the directions

Finally, I offered myself to the centre with the sound '-uu'. As I ran out of breath on the '-uu' sound I touched my forehead to the forehead of the Buffalo.

the centre

The presence of the Buffalo is doing something for my throat centre, I don't know how that will progress but I definitely feel the spirit energy approaching my throat. There is also a lot of activity in my centre of seeing but I do feel that the Buffalo connection is something that exists primarily in the heart and the solar plexus, and that it is a joining together of those two energy centres. I feel that it is a major event in my life.

After the ceremonies of the heart and of the solar plexus, I found that, having given them to the Buffalo, the spirit world made changes to me and awakened abilities in those centres.

The Spirit House of the Buffalo

I have thought deeply about the people who participated in sending me the gift of the Buffalo skull and specifically about the person who killed the Buffalo. I have prayed for them and I feel I have a connection with them. I was taken in meditation to a place called the spirit house of the Buffalo; a square lodge, the walls of which were buffalo skin, and I met those people. I felt that they saw me. I went again today, because I liked it so much, but when I got there, spirit lights kept hitting me and I couldn't see anything; the lights entirely disrupted my ability to concentrate.

This morning there was more solar plexus work. It was pretty painful and difficult. I was struggling, seeking to formulate visions, something I don't normally do, but making the attempt was an essential part of understanding the opening of the solar plexus. Then I heard, spoken very strongly: "Be at peace!" and I was able to enter a state of peace with the Buffalo skull in my solar plexus, reaching a state similar to the one I had felt in my heart, and then, without effort, vision began. The next thing I remember was stuffing the nose of the Buffalo skull with red material and I decided: "Yes, I must do that. Maybe also I should put the colour blue into the eye sockets."

I felt very peculiar at the end of this meditation, I was clumsy, and, both before and afterwards, I felt extremely dizzy. The Buffalo seemed to have shrunk to a tiny thing and I seemed to have got very big. I covered the skull and went to the village to get some bread. When I came back, thinking I would wash the kitchen floor, do something practical after all this spirit work, I was hit physically with the wobbles and dizziness. I laid myself down and a great whoosh of energy left me that made me shake, so I knew I must return to travelling with the Buffalo.

We travelled through the navel centre, the solar plexus, and the heart, travelling in feeling and connecting together. I had a visionary experience where they said: "Look up." I looked up, and above me, I saw columns of crystal, cliffs of crystal, mountains of crystal, stretching ever upwards. I heard: "Those are the teachings that are coming." I understood that they were coming through the Buffalo skull and that not all these teachings would be directly transmitted through me, but through contact with the Buffalo, other people would receive different aspects of them, because these mountains were vast. It was the most beautiful sight to look up at all the crystal visions and I stayed with that for a long time.

Then I moved; the colour was red. Red was everywhere and filled everything and I understood why I put red into the mouth of the Buffalo. Why Red? This is an initiation. I was spoken to a lot today, given very kind and very good advice. I was able to speak too. At one point, I heard a sentence coming: "You will get your rewards." The mention of rewards always makes me feel that expecting them could make my motivation wrong. I don't need the rewards. That is true; I do this for love. I do it for LOVE! And saying that is having the same effect on me now as it did when I said it then, I am crying.

A Sacred Knot

I have just completed a perfect ceremony with the skull of the Buffalo, which looked so beautiful this morning when I took the cloths off. Last night the Power was so strong and so shattering that I covered the skull up; it didn't make the slightest difference because all the Power still came through. I had reached the stage of complete insomnia and just lay there all night in a state of mental awareness without anything much appearing to happen, perhaps because so much had happened before.

This morning I lay with my head against the four-stranded plait in the Buffalo's nose. The colour Black flowed into me, I acknowledged it, saying: "-ii," very carefully, and then I sang the sound: "-ii," very loudly, with all the breath that I had, and the awareness of the colour Black poured in more strongly, flowing all the way down the centre of my Being right to the root of my root centre.

The colour White appeared to the left of the Black and placed in me the sensation of whiteness and I moved to the sound: "-eh," saying it and then singing it. The colour Yellow appeared to the right of the Black and my body was washed with the colour energy of Yellow, I said and sang: "-ah." The three colours came to rest beside one another below the solar plexus. Then the colour Red rose above them and condensed into a great ball, filling the solar plexus, while the other colours wove a three-stranded plait below. Being taught by the colour Red, I spoke and sang: "-oh."

The four colours and sounds of the directions were in place and I moved to the centre of the medicine wheel, saying: "-uu." Blue was the colour and my heart was the centre. I sang the sound:

"-uu" and, as I sang, the Blue expanded upwards to my centre of seeing and my head opened with the sound of '-uu'. I saw myself as a blue light with a red knot below and below that the black, white, and yellow strands of a plait. The four colours below the blue heaved and moved in my body, my body was the engine of their expression, above them the colour blue was the place of being-aware-in-clarity.

a sacred knot

The Blue Buffalo

In my meditation the Buffalo skull immediately laid the Power upon me, every part of my aura was fizzing, the image was blue and I knew that I must follow the blue. Surrounded by blue, blue sky, I found myself looking at the largest rock on Earth, Uluru, in the Red Centre of Australia. I entered in and saw, knocked into the ground at a slight angle, a post with a flat top. I thought: "That is just the sort of place an owl would perch." Immediately an owl came and perched there. How delightful!

We moved in unison, the owl flapped its wings, I took a step and I was sucked up off the ground into its body. Merged together, we flew to a triangular cleft in the orange rock. I went through the cleft into a great temple. Ahead of me, seated on a throne, was an immensely tall Blue Buffalo spirit Being. That spirit was eighty times bigger than I was and I was awe-struck: there was no doubt that I was in the presence of Greatness and I prayed: "Oh Great Spirit, take me in." My request was granted. The Blueness expanded to fill the cave and took me in, a most wonderful feeling.

I came next to a cave eroded by the wind and I passed through this cave into a black land. There I met my Buffalo in all his brown and earthly glory, but this was the land-beyond-life and the light was black. I stood beside the beautiful Buffalo with my arm upon his shoulder while he ate the green grasses that grew there in the darkness, just a few grasses there.

After that, Time stopped and there is a blank. When my awareness came back, I was watching Eagles flying in a clear blue sky. It was wonderful to see them flying again; they were the Eagles killed by road-trains on the road to Alice Springs.

It is the case that I was given the opportunity by the spirits to dance to the Eagle and the Buffalo at the Sun Moon Dance in the UK. Then Eagles came to me four months later in Australia after the first Sun Moon Dance in the southern hemisphere, came, some alive, some dead, as my Teacher and I travelled through the Red Centre on our way to the greatest Rock, Uluru. Now, the Buffalo skull has come to me. Yes, these are the wonderful things that happen. Um...... I don't know what else to say.

New Year

The Long Road

This morning's meditative journey began somewhere near the beginning with myself having to take a walk down a long road. Wishing for a companion, I asked: "Who will walk down this road with me?" The Brown Buffalo came to stand by my right shoulder, his foreleg and shoulder were the size of my entire body, and we began to walk. As we walked, I knew the Buffalo would carry me and I rolled up into a ball and disappeared inside him.

In that place of safety I had the opportunity to detach myself from the pain that I am feeling at the thought of leaving the deep, close, free contact I have had with the Buffalo for so many days. This pain has to be sealed as I am going to my father's house to celebrate the Millennium. The Buffalo skull is not going and I felt it should be covered while I am away. After the meditation, I put on the wrappings. It seemed very important that I did this in a good way: only time will tell if I did it correctly or not. It is done for my own sake. Yes, the spirit world is all right: nothing much is a problem to them.

The Black Buffalo

On the journey to visit my father I bled; I menstruated. It was unexpected and I couldn't believe what I was seeing because I felt that my bleeding times were close to an end. I had not bled since the Dance six months ago. It is true that ceremonial work often brings on a woman's moon-time. I don't know why that is, but it feels like the bleeding is part of the power of the work. I had thought: "Oh, as I get older it must have to be some other process because bleeding is no longer likely." Now, as a result of the work with the Buffalo, it has happened.

I have to say that when I meditated on the Buffalo at my

father's house, it was visible to me, but very, very small, very, very black, and very, very powerful. Set high up in the left-hand side of my mind, it was about the size of a postage stamp stuck on a very large envelope. The things that impressed me were its minute compactness and its pitch blackness. Last night, back at home, I meditated with the Buffalo skull and the experience wasn't all beautiful, lovely, pleasant feelings, but it was powerful and I surrendered, without memory, to where it would take me.

This morning that Black Buffalo was standing in front of me very, very huge. It just stood there. Everything was very slow and still and very intense. Eventually I took the skull and laid it on my chest. The Black Buffalo came closer and I asked it to lead me to the Great Spirit, and I asked it to show me how to pray, and how to make myself available for whatever needed to be done.

In the Spirit Lodge

At the end of the long Christmas holiday, I needed to change my relationship to Time in order to be able to go back to running my business. As I rested before going to sleep the Buffalo came, his colour was brown with blackish tinges on the thicker coat around his shoulders. He walked slowly on my right-hand side taking me with him. We entered a cave where he showed me the images of european bison painted on the walls by neolithic hunters, and it struck me how many thousands of years humans have been in a relationship with bison. Although he was waiting for me to go further, I was too tired and I didn't make it.

I got up this morning, fetched the Buffalo skull and came to meditate with it. When I had woken up earlier, I had a pain in my navel centre, not an excitement, but an aching, maybe the skull could ease this pain. I placed the Buffalo skull on my body and it sank into my womb where the red blood drenched it and I remembered how the bison's blood had poured out over me, the hunter, in a vision the previous summer. I felt that was why I bled now, to return the blood, and I lay with the Buffalo skull while it received the colour red from my body. When all of the red had been released, the colours black and green were left. The green was growing in the blackness of my nature, that aspect of creativity had been found, released, and activated in me.

After a while, an overwhelming and confusing black spiritual presence came; I accepted that presence. I saw a stone with only a very small part of its surface area touching the flat ground on which it lay. Through this stone, I discovered that the black spirit was the Mother-of-lost-beginnings. I entered into her dark space.

There was a movement on the right, a shape emerged and rose up, curved over and became a skin-covered lodge. Inside, fixed at the height of my solar plexus on a T-shaped pole, was the skull of the Buffalo. I looked, I stared, and slowly I began to clothe the skull with flesh and hide. The face of the Buffalo emerged and then the entire body of the Buffalo was standing there.

I focused on the cloven hooves and, as I stared, I was drawn to become the ground beneath them. I felt all four of those hooves standing on my body; they were the four directions: North, East, South, and West. It was an extremely excellent feeling to have the four legs of the Buffalo planted on my body.

Seeing the tail, thin but tipped with a sturdy switch of long hairs, I reached out my hand and grabbed it. I travelled up the spine of the Buffalo, up, up, up, my awareness pressed against the brown skin. At the highest point I came to an opaque region that was a lighter colour, a faded moon colour, I had reached the smoke hole. My body passed across this hole and, as it did so, it became the skin of a drum. When the grey smoke and heat from the fire below hit the drum skin it dissolved and together they rose through the hole of the lodge into the sky. In that way I ascended and waited there, waited, waited; waited until the sky was blue and the Yellow Coyote came to bring me back to this place.

Spring

In the Peace Chamber

Tonight there happened to be a programme on TV about the Inca people and it showed how greatly their culture revered the Llama. The Llama, herbivore not predator, worthy of infinite respect, my modern mind asked: "Why? Aren't herbivores essentially powerless?"

I came upstairs to play the drum and, as I was playing, I heard the footfalls of a wolf in the drumbeat and I felt the buffalo become extremely alert and wary; the buffalo would keep the hungry wolf alive: the life of the wolf depended on the buffalo. I realized how way off the mark my interpretation of power, so clearly expressed a short while before, had been. The life of the Inca people had depended on the Llama; they knew that and they were grateful.

Thinking more deeply about the way that life is sustained by life I changed my attitude, and I placed the creatures whose lives feed life in the direction of the South on the medicine wheel. When I had done that, I understood why the colour White, the colour of placement, is so prominent in my spiritual quest. Whiteness filled my heart centre and that was beautiful; it is the place of Peace.

The meditation entered the great spirit spaces where things seem comprehensible but I can't hang onto them. Eventually I found the white skull of the Buffalo coming towards me. It came and lay upon me, energising my heart, my solar plexus, and my navel centre where the plait entered deep into my Being and dipped into an orange coloured pool that looked like rusty water. I wondered: "What's happening? What is this image?"

Then the skull said to me invitingly: "Come in, come in." I went in through the white bone forehead into a lodge which had curving walls but the space inside was not circular; it was oval. This lodge was an adobe construction and not a skin covered lodge of bent branches; close to the ceiling round pieces of wood stuck out from the walls like pegs. On these wooden pegs were hung Buffalo heads that still had their skin upon them. The Buffalo skull now hung at the end of this line and, being bone, it was the only one that was white.

Yesterday I asked this of a person I know who believes that menstruating women should not enter ceremonies: "If menstruation is inimical to the energy of ceremony why did I bleed in the work that I did with the Buffalo in the Sun Moon Dance and at Christmas?" She did not know, but, in my meditation, I remembered that I did know. It was because the Buffalo had bled so profusely for us. The moon-time blood is like bleeding for the Buffalo and there is a process of repaying a debt during those times. Then it came to me that menstrual bleeding is another of the ways in which life sustains life.

Through the Spirit Lodge

A few days later, during a seminar led by my Teacher, the group members journeyed to their upper worlds. The drumming began and I called to the Buffalo. I stood next to the big brown and black body of the Buffalo, our shoulders touched. We were standing here, in this world. Up in the sky was a large circular hole, which was held open by the horns of the Buffalo, a hole through which the Ancestors entered and exited. The Buffalo and I walked together, we rose up together, we went through this hole, and we stood together on the Great Plains. The view was endless, endless beauty, endless calm beauty. I stood there with the Buffalo and I took hold of his left horn, because I was standing, always, on his left-hand side.

I looked again across the Great Plain and some long distance away I noticed a brown mound; it was a lodge covered with a buffalo hide. I knew it was the Buffalo spirit lodge. I thought: "I have done this before. I can go straight there." I went straight there. I went straight inside. I thought: "I have done this before. I know how to travel from this lodge; I go through the smoke hole." I rose up through the smoke hole.

Above me I saw the panorama of the night sky and a voice said to me: "Find your Star." I went. If I wanted to describe the direction, up, ahead, and left of centre, that is where it would be. I travelled to the Star. I knew that I was travelling to see the Star Maiden who came to see me once and I lost ninety per cent of the memory of her visit, but she had come to Earth to visit me in a meditation and now I would go to visit her. I arrived at the Star and I entered in. It was composed of crystalline colours, which were the essence of the beautiful Being, who, as I entered, entered me and especially entered me in the area below my heart, entering all the energy centres there.

I felt the Ancestors arriving, coming in feeling into my body. They were a vast circular space that tingled on all the edges of my awareness, especially on the lower left-hand edge. This was the place where the Star Maiden had come into my perception.

When a certain point was reached, I was able to look more closely at the crystalline colours of light that composed the ancestral place. There was pink. I allowed the pink to enter my Being and move in me. The same thing happened again and the colour was mauve, then green and then blue. Golden-yellow was the last colour of the light to enter and I began to line them up in my body. I lined them up. I thought I would return to the Earth with the colours in this order: first pink, then mauve, green next, blue and, finally, golden-yellow. I would come to the Earth like a shooting star with these colours trailing.

But it was not the time in the journey to do that. I looked back down at the Great Plains and I saw the tiny spirit lodge standing there. I spoke to the Star Maiden: "I don't like some aspects of that place. Why do I sometimes get pestered and battered by all those spirit energies? And why is it so confusing?" I looked down from this place beyond, and the lodge appeared to me as a beehive full of Bees. That was an entirely appropriate image of the business of that place. Then I saw the honey in the hive and I seemed to understand that without the spirit lodge there would be no golden light perceivable below. I saw the black and yellow Bees and I connected the energies of the spirit lodge with the yellow and black colours that make the day and night, the two lights, the duality that makes our world.

As I continued to look at the beehive, I heard: "In this way you can ...." and three words followed. ..... Oh, I am not sure now what the words were! I know that 'be' was the last word because it was a pun on the Bees and I knew I wouldn't forget that word. As to the rest, I am not so sure. I think they were 'feel' and 'sense'. Yes, I am pretty sure that the three words were 'sense, feel and be', so the sentence was: "In this way you can sense, feel and be."

Then I returned to the essence of the Star Maiden, the Star Maiden who I am deeply in love with, who brings a certain ecstasy to my psyche that is available nowhere else, and I said to her: "Press farther into my Being. Push farther into my awareness." Because, until now, this great circle of ancestral awareness had only been in my lower centres. She answered my request; the crystalline colours began to push further up my body and they travelled up through my heart centre and into my brain. Somewhere deep in my brain in the back lobes on the right-hand side they came to a halt, or a barrier, or a blockage, or a density, or a, um, what could I call it? an obfuscation. This obstacle was black and, in the first moment, I was shocked to find the colour black here where the Star Maiden had penetrated with the light. Then I remembered: "But I like black. In fact, I love black, and I love to travel in the black light, and the black light teaches me many things." But there was some sense in which the essence of the Star Maiden and this blackness in my brain were not compatible.

The star light found this black place and I thought: "Do I need help in this place?" As I looked, purple light came, Joseph comes with purple light, and that was what was needed in this dark place. The darkness needed to be fused with the purple light in order for something to happen, in order for the next thing to happen? I don't know but the black and the purple met together, and they mixed. As that happened my head and then my body began to stretch in a great arc. My feet remained attached with the Star Maiden while my head and my body stretched like a great bow. They stretched and bowed, and travelled down towards the Great Plains, and I felt the black and purple lights enter first into the smoke hole of the Buffalo skin lodge. They entered in and the whole of my Being stretched out behind them. My feet were still attached to the Star and the colours radiated back from my head towards it: the purple, then the black, followed by the yellow, the blue, the green, the mauve, and finally, the pink, closest to the Star.

I stretched down like a night-bow in the sky, and then I was within the Buffalo lodge. The whole lodge collapsed and fell flat as if it was only a skin lying on the ground. Now this, maybe, was something that I thought might have been a good idea to get rid of all that pesky astral stuff. But as soon as the skin was lying flat on the ground, I realized that all connection between the worlds above and below was lost. I decided to reconstruct the lodge. I stood up inside it, in this way raising the roof and re-forming it into a mound shape. While I was doing that, the Buffalo came in physical form to collect me. We came back through the great hole in the sky. We stood again, here on the Earth, together.

I looked at my solar plexus; it was green and grass was growing there. I lay down on my back and I said to the Buffalo: "Eat. Eat the grass. Be nourished." The tongue of the Buffalo, which was quite purple, wrapped itself around the grass and pulled it from the ground. For the last few moments of the journey I watched the Buffalo chewing the grass, munching the grass right here on this plain, and that was something wonderful.

The Healing Guide

Last night when I came to bed and lay in a trance before sleeping pricking sensations in my body kept happening, particularly in my left leg. They were so painful that an involuntary leap of my leg would jerk me far away from the state that I was trying to enter.

This morning, entering meditation without pain, I heard: "Your body is the temple of your spiritual life." Then I began to travel. I found myself facing the North. The daunting Spirit of the North was standing there. A cleft opened up in my body and the furrow it made was full of green-ness. The Brown Buffalo came walking along the furrow and, stopping at the solar plexus, lowered his head to eat the grass. As his tongue wrapped round the green the colour of the Buffalo changed to red. The red began to drip, drip, drip and to penetrate my Being. I heard that when the Buffalo ate the grass that I made it did not damage me, but when I had taken what the Buffalo offered I had killed it entirely.

I became a Wolf searching the Great Plains. I found the living spirit Buffalo and I began to tear at its coat. It was as if I was shaking it to wake up, but I was ripping it apart. The power of this image was intense and as I, in the form of the ravenous Wolf, ate the Buffalo, I asked myself would I ever become so peaceful that I was the Buffalo and not the Wolf?

I will try to recall some of the journey that I took while attending a weekend seminar locally. The seminar was led by a kind woman from the Seneca Wolf Clan, she had recorded her instructions with accompanying music and we were to take a journey to meet our healing guide. I am not used to travelling in this way as usually I travel in silent meditation or to the sound of a drum. I find it amazing that I managed to take such a powerful healing journey against the background of a pre-recorded guided meditation which I fought every step of the way.

As the music began, the Black Coyote came. I welcomed him with such joy; I felt certain he was my healing guide. I looked at his dark form and deep into his green eyes and we began to travel. We met the Yellow Coyote at a certain point and then we three, the black and the yellow and the white, twisted together in a powerful vortex. My consciousness began moving down my body, down through my generative and root centres into the void that exists below.

In the void, we became luminous fibres like little worms. These luminous fibres wanted to travel on and I noticed that the spirits deeply approved of this form of being for me, but the guided journey worked against it, and while the luminous fibres were busy forming a spherical ball the voice of the guided journey suddenly said that we were standing on the Great Plains. My consciousness left the ball of fibres and rose into the emptiness of a dark sky.

I heard the recorded voice talking about green grass and I said: "Yes, I will stand on the green grass of the Great Plains." I looked down and saw my feet just touching the grass. The voice began to talk about a doorway. Well, yes, there was a square opening, but it certainly had no door in it. I stood looking at this entrance thinking: "Well, now I am here" when a spirit voice said: "Step in," and I realized: "Now I have reached my hidden healing guide." The only thing I had to do was make the effort to go in.

I stepped through into the presence of the Blue Buffalo spirit. How beautiful to find that spirit there as a deep, deep healing guide. He was in the form of a Being with the head, horns and the deep curly locks of the Buffalo and a man's body below, so strong and so beautiful. I was a tiny blue spherical light. I laughed at the fact that the form of the Great Spirit was so comprehensible while I was simply a small blue light.

I travelled to the horns of the Great Buffalo. When I touched them, the most overwhelming sensation of the unconditional love emanating from the presence of the Blue Spirit filled me and the journey assumed a childlike aspect: I used the horns as slides, up I climbed and down I slid. I was so happy that the thought of returning to the world of everyday caused me to cry out: "I can't take the pain of going back."

This was understood, and, in return, I understood that I should enjoy and appreciate the experience while it lasted and not worry about the pain of the return. I did do that and spent a very wonderful time with the spirit of the Blue Buffalo. There was an unfamiliar image of a white alabaster boat-shaped object, which was my self, and resting within it was a blue sphere that very gently rolled back and forth.

Then the Blue Spirit sucked me into his mouth and blew me out as a cloud. I travelled as a cloud. Then I travelled as a white bird. Then I travelled as a polar bear. I went into a white fox. As I changed into the forms that the Buffalo spirit was sending me through I realized that this was the way to take away the pain of the return. From the white fox, I went through the form of a white mouse. Then I went through the form of a little white star-shaped flower.

Suddenly I was back on the Great Plains. The talking of the journey was winding to a close. I heard the voice instruct me to bathe my eyes in clear water, but the Coyotes came and dragged me through a mud pool. I was laughing my head off that they behaved so contrary to the instructions. In the mud, we had a wrestling match and that was good because it brought me back into a love of my body and back into the room with only a few tears in my eyes.

In Deep Water

A few weeks later, I hurt my back re-stacking a woodpile that I felt someone else had stacked badly. The next day at work my muscles were in spasm and when I lay down at teatime to reduce the pressure the pain was astronomical. Luckily, it eased off in the evening and I had a reasonably good night's sleep. I have to blame myself: the injury was caused by my unreasonable anger, anger that turned round and hurt only me.

Yes, I have been making a few mistakes lately because my

present life is breaking up, and when I come to meditate, I tend to drift into dreams about where I am going to live when I move. I realize that it is all-important to me to have a secure base. It is a time of turmoil. I played my drum for the spirits last night, but I didn't ask them to heal me because I knew it was completely my own fault and I should take the consequences.

When I came to meditate this morning, it wasn't very long before I remembered what I had been trying to remember as I struggled with the pain yesterday: the journey at the seminar a few weeks ago. After I had made the recording, the details had left my mind completely. Very swiftly the spirit, the beautiful and overwhelmingly welcoming spirit, of the Blue Buffalo came. After I had dwelt in that healing radiance for a while, I entered the colour green and I rested in the Grasslands waiting for pictures.

When I looked up, I saw the flat surface of an ocean that was just within my reach. I went to the shore and I looked out across the silver dappled surface of this vast expanse of water. Breaking the surface a Dolphin came, calling: "Come into the depths of the ocean with me." I longed to do that. I loved this Dolphin, I loved the energy, youthful enthusiasm, and lack of, um, traumatic individuality. I waded into the sea, and, speaking frankly, I just wanted closer contact. The Dolphin touched me lightly and said: "It is far more fun to swim into the deeper ocean."

I became a dolphin and we swam away from the shore. Though now completely supported by the water, I still wanted physical contact and I wondered: "Could our flippers touch as we swim?" The Dolphin laughed and said: "We are connected in our minds, and when we swim together, and move together, and jump together as a pair, or even in a big group, we are one thing. Carried by the water, we do not crave contact."

We swam on, scattering myriads of silver drops as we leapt through the water, and that is when I remembered that light can turn the surface of the ocean into a mirror. Diving through the mirror into the depths, we came into a silver space and there, floating upright in the water, we paused. We opened up our navel centres and the silver energy, or light, or essence, or power, flowed into us. I went with the feeling and allowed the power of silver to enter me and change my perception.

How can it be then that? Ah, yes, I began to become aware of the attentive silver-grey mare of the Ancient Grandfather. In fact, the head and neck of this horse were sticking out of my solar plexus. Hum, was I becoming her? Or was she becoming out of me? These questions were academic: I was one with the horse, and we were pointing West.

The Grandfather pulled the horse's head to the right and encouraged her to run. We ran to the North. He pulled the rein again and she turned a complete circle on the spot that was the North. Then, at a signal from the Grandfather, she ran to the East and did the same. The speed got faster and faster. She ran to the South and, by the skill of the Grandfather, turned through the complete circle there. She ran to the West and the same thing was done. Four circles on the spot and one circuit of the medicine wheel had been run.

Then the Grandfather turned the horse's head towards the North again, and I saw a herd of buffalo, thousands strong, running round the circle of the medicine wheel. They ran and we ran in among them. Now I too was a person on a horse in among the thundering mass of black and brown coloured buffalo. Among them, I saw the White Buffalo. I knew the White Buffalo would take me to the centre and I leapt onto her back. She ran to the very centre of the medicine wheel and stopped.

Everything was still and the colour was silver-white except for the blue eyes of the Buffalo. I began to sink; the colour Red came from all directions and covered me. I was descending a level in the medicine wheel; I was going down into the North below.

I came, for the second time, into an appreciation of my ancientness in the form of a red, triangular Being, but as my recording of it on this occasion is sketchy on the tape, I have placed the original encounter, which happened some time ago, here:

I was swimming in the great oceanic void. I began to chant the vowel sounds from the name of the Spirit of the Oceans, Oceanus: "-oh, -ii, -ah, -uu; -oh, -ii, -ah, -uu." Listening to the sounds I realized that one sound, '-eh', placement, was missing and I became a plankton creature floating.

Eventually on the deepest, deepest part of the ocean floor, I spied something. It was a seated, red figure hunched over a blue light, but both the figure and the light were flames, a flame of red and a flame of blue. How did flames burn at the deep bottom of the ocean sea? I approached and I became into the shape of the seated figure, a red soft-edged triangle.

To call that figure 'I' would be wrong because my 'I' was only a part of that consciousness, but 'I' wished to lift the blue flame, and as I did so the flame became a sphere which I put into the solar plexus. I saw that other colours were already present. The colour white was two small dots, one in the eye and one in the throat. The colour green was located between the solar plexus and the heart. The heart was a yellow sphere.

the oceanic being

    I had entered fully into the being-ness of this Being and .... what on earth happened then? .... I can't remember. Maybe I reconnected to that Being and found out where its place is in relation to everything else: in the depths of ancientness before the time of now. I don't remember, but somewhere, surely in the silver light of the ocean when I swam as a dolphin before the power overwhelmed me, I saw a hammerhead shark and I heard: "Here is an example of the creative energy of the Power. Look at this creature. How could anything be imagined to be made that was like that?" In this way, I learned that the Power is greater than the imagination.

In Deep Earth

    Oh difficult, difficult woman that-I-can't-get-on-with! The only way I could get rid of her horrible invasive psychic poison cloud was to dive into the earth. I dove in, feeling her, being only a wind storm, unable to penetrate the surface. I went deeper and I became a white earthworm travelling at speed through the ground. She was like a blackbird banging on the surface and pecking at the ground trying to call the earthworm up. But this earthworm was too damn smart. It went deeper, and deeper, and deeper.

As I travelled, I noticed that each grain of earth was brown and surrounded by space. The space between them was getting bigger and in this space, particles of golden dust drifted which gave off light. I began to collect the specks of golden dust by rolling among them to catch them on my sticky skin and pulling them into my body.

I broke through a tremendous, terrible, horrible barrier that was composed of the colour Red. All the death, the violence and the blood, the agony, the pain, the suffering, how could these things be the spiritual colour of the North, which is Red? I broke my way through this northern barrier and came to a place that was still a brown earth place but that also had a grainy whiteness to it, like grains of chalk. Brown and white it was, speckled, and then I came into an open plain deep within the Earth.

I saw clearly a herd of animals. Strangely, even though they were scattered about on the plain, they all stood pointing in one direction. I chose one to focus on, I saw it in detail and I spent a very long time trying to decide what it might be. As far as I know it is not an animal that exists in our world now but it was like a very short-legged bison that had a long back. The head was set up higher than a buffalo in a straight line with the shoulders and, although the front shoulders were stocky, they were nowhere near the size of the shoulders of an american bison. It had a tail that was like a buffalo tail, but it was much shorter and only just covered the anus. It had cloven hooves. Its coat was greenish-brown and shaggy, but it was not thick. When I came to the head, I saw that the horns were most like the horns of a ram. They were spiral and they curled downwards, growing close to the sides of the head.

Now I touched foreheads with this animal, it flipped me up and I did a somersault. I landed on its back and I began to amalgamate with it. I went into a place of retreat and complete safety within this creature. "Bos Primogenitor" is what, in a scientific moment, I called it. I have to say that I did not see it walk; it never moved from the spot that it was standing on. I have entered into it for a long period of time and I love it deeply. In there I was able to stand quite quietly without any thoughts. Yes, I enjoyed the contact with the deep earth bovine.

The Silver Streams

When I came to bed last night, some important things happened. As I woke this morning, I had vague awareness of them but could not clearly recall a thing. I entered the meditative state trying once more to recall the experiences. I felt a great opening of my navel centre. Then the awareness rose up and my attention became concentrated in my centre of seeing. The energy then split itself so that I had awareness in my belly and in my eye of seeing at the same time. I began to travel.

I saw the mound of the Buffalo skin lodge ahead of me. I went in. The lodge was vast inside but I couldn't see anybody. I know it is always full of spirits but I couldn't see any. I went straight to the centre, it too was empty, there was no fire burning there. I bent down and struck my forehead against the ground right in the very centre of the pit.

It was like striking a match and I became two curls of smoke, one white, one grey. The curls rose up through the hole in the roof and I was on the Great Plains. I looked around, still in the form of smoke, and I began to think about my daily life, about work, about a customer's job. How should I organise it? What would I do next? These thoughts happened without taking me away from the spirit place, but I was amazed that I allowed them to be there.

I dropped them and brought my attention back to the Great Plain where I saw many grazing buffalo. I chose one, a female. She was contemplatively chewing the cud. I went and stood beside her, nothing much was going on, everything was very peaceful and tranquil and so I sat down on the ground.

It was then that I noticed a stream close by, it ran in many silver rivulets; it was like the diagrams that you see of the nervous system in human Beings. I laid my spirit body in the silver streams. I noticed that the current ran from my feet upwards, and, contrary to my expectation, I observed that the streams were running downhill, even though they were going, what would generally be considered to be, upwards in my body towards the head. The Buffalo was still near me. She did not move.

As I lay in the streams, I became more aware of my spirit body. The central section, where my energy centres of travelling are, became a rectangular box, longer than it was wide. This box had no lid. I put my hand in and pulled out the jug that sits on the windowsill in my present house. I felt exhausted and expressed my feelings: "I don't want to keep pulling things out of this box and looking at them. I will not take anything else out of the box."

I felt immense relief and I realized that I was lying in the landscape of the bungalow in Scotland that I would like to buy. The box was the bungalow, and the water in which I had laid my body was the burn that runs down the side of the garden. They were all in their exact geographical positions relative to their world. As I discovered this, a voice said: "The metaphor is established." Oh, I, I felt ...., I hoped to goodness it was true that I would buy this bungalow and that I could be free of clutter there.

The Coyote came to help me and we travelled to many places together while I gave up the pains that I have. I feel relaxed and happy now, and I came back thinking about whether to offer the Buffalo skull to hang on the Tree at the coming Sun Moon Dance, the second in the UK.

It was yesterday that the information came with the news that there will be a drumming and singing seminar after the Dance. I got so excited I nearly blew a fuse. I rang my Teacher and had a conversation with him that was so interesting and made me feel so connected that when I came off the phone I was almost unable to be in the everyday work energy. I began to get a headache and to feel sick. I had to be very careful because that went on all day. Oh, the conflict is quite difficult to cope with. To stay happy to be doing what I am doing; this is what must be done. Oh, eternal challenges of relative reality. .... Well, perhaps not eternal, just endless!

Dream of Running Buffalo

I had a very strange night's sleep, full of dreams and contacts with a spirit plain that was more like, what I call 'the random astral plain'. As I remember, the things that happened there weren't particularly nice, and were rather challenging.

I woke with this dream: I was driving along a road on the left-hand side. A very high bank to my left overhung the road, but the ground was level with the road surface on the right. From the left, I heard a familiar rumbling noise, the thunder of a herd of buffalo. I was completely amazed: "Where are buffalo coming from? This isn't even America."

I pulled the car over and stopped under the shelter of the bank. Coming from the higher ground, they leapt over the road and hit the other side running. The ginger-coloured herd were bunched so tightly together I was surprised that they didn't fall as they jumped the road and they just kept on coming; I can't imagine how many there were. I looked up at them hurtling overhead and I struggled to keep my eyes open. My eyes shut. I began to go into a trance-like state, I said to myself: "This is the only time you will ever see this! Keep your eyes open!" But something else said: "This is the only time you will ever experience this, keep your eyes shut!"

Eventually they were gone, disappearing rapidly into the distance. I found the car very difficult to drive after this. It had sunk a bit into the ground and I couldn't get it into gear. I managed to get into reverse gear, but then I couldn't remember which foot pedal was the brake. It all got very dangerous; the car hurtled onto the grass and ran out of control. Somehow, I managed to bring it to a stop.

Across the road, on the other side of a large field, I noticed a housing estate. The herd must have run right through it. I got out of the car and looked at the ground and, yes, I could see the swathe of hoof prints running from where they had landed and taking a curving track away to the right and through all the streets around these houses. There were a few people knocking about, but none of them seemed to have seen anything. I didn't like to ask because they were all behaving very normally and nothing like that could have possibly happened to them.

As I drove away, I was still struggling with the mechanics of the car. It was becoming so difficult to drive that I pulled over to sort out, well, the cushion I was sitting on, actually, but I don't know how that would have helped.

Where to Teeter?

I was lying here now thinking how beautiful it is to be taught by the beautiful spirits. Even though this is a period of change, the teaching still comes. Recently I had been feeling that I might have to wait till I was settled in Scotland before I could meditate intensely again, when I heard the words: "Not then, now!"

'Then' was when I thought I would be settled in the new place, and 'now' is the timeless moment. I contemplated 'now' and the vowels from this word, '-ah -uu', made a circuit of the medicine wheel ending up in the centre and leaving an open triangular section in the North East. I remembered Joseph's teaching, which tells how the founding spirits came to Earth from the North East. The opening into the '-ah -uu', our world, had the word 'Entrance' written next to it but which meaning did the word have: 'entrance' or 'en-trance'? No matter, in the timeless moment there is no time, and no need to make a choice.

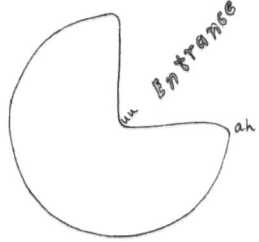

en-trance

I approached a barrier, which was grey, and I experienced a moment when I felt that I could not get through on my own. I called out, hoping, but not sure, that the Coyotes would come to help me, and they did come, the Yellow one on the left and the Black one on the right. They were strong, immovable. I braced myself against them and, pushing against the doorjambs the Coyotes made, I burst through the grey barrier. I could not possibly have gone through without them; I could not have generated the force required on my own.

Ahead I saw a blue point of light and I travelled towards it knowing that I was going to the Blue Buffalo spirit. I arrived. I don't know why that spirit is buried so deep within the darkness of the underworld, but it is. Today it was a cave full of blue light, and, on arriving there, I was handed a green light in the shape of a drip of water.

I suppose that the specific gravity, which holds the drip together, makes that marvellous bulbous shape, the lower end hanging down, curved and fat, the top end narrowing into an elongating point. I licked the convex surface of this inviting drop and my tongue felt the surface tension and the viscosity that kept it in one lick-able piece. Even though it could be broken into many drops, my lick did not break it, and that showed me the strength of its cohesion. The green drop entered me.

From some distance away, outside my body, I watched the green drop travelling into my heart centre. The image was of the blackness-that-is-matter surrounded by the green drop while both were held by the encircling blue. My will was the green drop, so attracted to the place of creativity, so strong in self-containment yet fragile, always longing to be absorbed into the one vast drop of consciousness, the blue.

I came back from this journey to an appreciation of ecstasy in my navel centre such as I felt when I uncovered the Buffalo skull and saw it again after many days of being covered. I felt this ecstasy and a voice said to me: "You can have the ecstasy and the pain, or you can just have the pain. It is in your programme." I understood. I had been brought up and shaped in this life to reject the ecstasy and cling to the pain, was this in any way sensible? Or what a sane person would choose? No. And I determined to overcome my addiction to pain as a place of safety where things teeter on the verge of getting worse, and to try and attach myself to the ecstasy that is available teetering on the edge of things getting better, choosing to be obliterated by better-ness and not by worse-ness. The thought of being obliterated is very scary, but surely it is better to go the ecstasy way? And in that way I came back here.

The other thing that I need to mention is that yesterday I got a letter from the solicitor saying that my offer for the bungalow is accepted. The letter contained a long document full of horror, terror, sewage discharge, asbestos certificates, no record of access to the water supply, etcetera. But I have determined to ignore all the potential problems and get the sale completed.

Moving North

Something very spectacular happened during the night with the power of the Ancient Grandfather pouring into me. I was in a state of consciousness where it was fairly easy for me to open up to the incomprehensible and to observe it do whatever was necessary. I woke from sleep to this experience and I marvelled at how easy it was to stick with it on waking like that, whereas sometimes when I am meditating it is so hard.

When I got up this morning, I felt quite strange and I hoped I would be brought to a state where I could function in my life. I had faith in that as I began to meditate. The Grandfather returned and I tried, in the state of consciousness that I have at this time of the day, to go to the same state of consciousness that I was in during the night. It was not easy.

The power of this Grandfather was very disturbing, very breaking up of all my familiar knowing. It was a struggle to accept this new way of perceiving. The pineal gland was pulsating and sending out chemicals through all of my Being to change me; my mind expanded and my consciousness focused on accepting. Everything became calm; there was no longer a struggle. I had reached a state of resting awareness.

Another Grandfather came, not the Ancient Grandfather whose colour is Grey; this Grandfather's colour was Black. He came behind me and pulled my spine against his body, I have to call it a 'body', as my back touched his body I realized he was the daunting Spirit of the North. From his blackness came blue and red, he sent the blue into my heart centre and the red into my mind centre, and these two colours were radiating through me from behind.

Held by the Northern Grandfather I looked forwards through the blue and red energies and I saw ahead of me the pitch Black Buffalo. It was standing, black in the blackness, and I, illuminated by the red and blue, stood aware of it in that place. For a long, long time I looked at it and it looked steadily at me.

Summer

The Necessity of Falling

Yesterday the purchase of the bungalow went through five minutes before the solicitors' offices closed. Yes, I felt I had to push to get it done. I had pushed and it was done. Now I must wait for a buyer for my old house. Then I can close up my present life and move north, meantime I can only pay swift visits at the weekends to my new place.

I came to meditate this morning and immediately I felt the Buffalo presence at my back. She was full size and brown. She pushed me gently forwards. She pushed me onto my knees. I didn't want to fall and be crushed by the Buffalo, but if I resisted I would simply live my normal life, so I did fall onto my knees. Then she pushed me onto my front so that my belly lay against the ground and she stood upon me. Then she lay upon me so that there was no chance of my moving and she stayed there for the whole of this meditation. When I checked it out, there she was holding me still in place, and that was good.

I lay with my belly against the ground and I looked into the earth realm. First of all I was acutely aware of the male energy of the earth and then the female energy came; the female energy occupied the major space of the brown earth, nevertheless there was male energy present, existing and part of the whole; together these two great black-brown Spirits of the Land make up the crust of the planet.

They gave me a gift. They put into my psyche the horizontal trunk of a tall Pine Tree. What was the trunk of a Pine Tree doing lying in the earth? I immediately wanted to rearrange this vision, but when I tried to move it and make the Pine Tree grow up from the surface, the power of the journey died. I had to come back to the dark earth place where the she-Buffalo held me, and I had to investigate the gift that the earth Beings were giving me, a vision of the Pine Tree horizontal.

As I looked at it, I began to think about the nature of gifts and how they are teachings because they bring an input from the giver, so, what teaching were the earth Beings giving me? I looked closer at the Tree, the needles were greenish-blue and the bark had a greenish-yellow tinge. The bark was marked by curved lines running horizontally that were caused by tiny sharp points. Because of these twig-like extrusions, the outer surface was prickly but, although it might be uncomfortable to fold myself around it, I determined to take it into my body, and I did this. Within my body, the Tree became vertical and I carefully inspected its effect there. The diameter of the trunk filled the circle of my navel centre but it did not take even a sixth of the space that was in my heart centre. Then I looked at it in my solar plexus.

Not able to grasp the teaching, I called to the Coyotes to help me. They came horizontally, Black and Yellow, as the teeth of a buzz saw. To my shock, at the height of the solar plexus they cut into the trunk of the Tree and sliced it in half. For a moment the top half balanced and I could see a crack of golden light where the coyote-saw had sliced through, I looked into that crack and the inside of the Tree was full of golden energy. I recalled that I had seen golden energy hidden among the earth particles and I understood that trees draw that energy into themselves as they reach up from the surface of the planet. Next minute the top section toppled over and the horizontal golden surface of the lower part was exposed. The cut end of the top section was still emitting golden light and looked rather like a tunnel, whereas the lower part looked more like a table.

A cabbage white butterfly landed on the table-like surface; it was going to drink the sap of the tree. As I watched the delicate proboscis uncurl, my body changed; the four wings of the butterfly became my arms and legs, and the body became my spine. I could feel the large wings beat and see the small body suspended between them. I wondered: "Is it possible that the fluttering of a single butterfly affects the entire world?" At that moment, there was a major spiritual transformation, and I became intensely aware of the Blue Buffalo spirit.

How surprised and happy I was to have reached the presence of this Being. But, if I entered in, I knew that I would lose the memory of all that had gone before. I havered there, trying to appreciate the beauty of the Blue Spirit and delight in the magnetic attraction which made me long to be absorbed within him, while trying also to satisfy the need to recall the journey for further inspiration. As I dallied, I began to lose the feeling of the presence of the Blue Buffalo and it was a hard choice. My happiness would rather have taken entry into the blueness, but I am so unhappy when I return and the details have disappeared that I did pause and place the journey up to that point in my memory.

Then I looked again for the Blue Spirit. After an intense search, I did find him at a particular place in my body and I entered in. Was it quite the same as the initial surrender would have been? I don't know, but it was beautiful. The Blue Buffalo spirit fills me with ecstatic joyfulness. However strange it is to my modern life mind to wish to maintain this connection, I need to do it or my life is a desert. After a while, I began to return. I tried to bring the presence of the Blue Buffalo spirit with me, but at a certain point as I returned the colour changed to jet black.

Calling

At the beginning of this meditation, I saw the Dance Chief in a golden light body burning like a clear, still flame. He was calling me as a dancer; he was looking to me as someone who is coming to fast, to pray and to dance.

The skull of the Buffalo was lying in the medicine tent. I went through the Buffalo and into the earth, a beautiful place of deep safety where Beings do not interfere with each other. It is safe because most people do not want to come into that place. The earth is so strong, so embracing, and so still that it is a place of knowing and being. I heard the qualities of the energy centres: the eye centre, all that can be seen; the solar plexus, all that can be felt; the navel centre, all that can be consumed; the heart centre, all that can be manifested.

Next time I shut my eyes the Buffalo skull was clear and present. I curled myself up into a ball. From this ball, which was made of the blackness of the sphere that was my self, four lines shot out and attached themselves to the top and bases of the horns; a spider's web was stretched between the horns and suspended in it was a black spider. I looked through this web and I saw the Northern Grandfather.

The blackness increased and I saw the guardians of the direction West: the dark Grandmother and Grandfather who are the energies of the Land. I made a quick decision, if I was going to learn about them today I would choose to learn about the Grandmother.

Slowly, slowly, through my navel centre, she revealed herself to me. I knew I was created out of this Mother and that in my life I was still within her womb being fed through the umbilical cord all of the energy I needed in order to live. I was quietly calling to her: "Feed me, feed me, feed me." I saw her smiling face, a deep, calm, constant, loving, beaming face. She is the Grandmother who smiles; she is the dark Mother-of-lost-beginnings. I stayed with her for a long, long time, experiencing different aspects of being nurtured in the quietness and peace of the dark earth.

I was still with her when the brown she-Buffalo came to lick my navel and solar plexus centres with her rough purple tongue. And I heard that for every Buffalo that was slaughtered on the plains there was a human Being who could be, and indeed was, connected to the Buffalo spirit, and who would, or could, awake now to do the work. I wondered how many people that was. I knew I was one of them.

Supporting the World

My meditation this morning began with the clear feeling that no matter what happened I should not hold up the journey because of my personal ideas. I began to see the Grandfathers. The Northern Grandfather called me strongly. I wanted to be with the Ancient Grandfather, but this want was clearly contrary to what I had agreed when I entered, so I put it aside, and I went with the pictures that were coming in.

I went to the Northern Grandfather who had the form of the shaft of a spear. At the top of the spear was a small triangular spearhead, looking like a black mountain, and so I named him 'Grandfather of the Black Mountain'. My solar plexus became an open circle and I saw the colour green. But, as I went towards this circle of green-ness, the Buffalo came and, being its living self, filled everything with brown-ness. I put my forehead against the head of the Buffalo and prayed.

I felt the experience wasn't finished and I did want to remember what had happened till now, so I went into the process of fixing the memory working backwards. When that was done, I returned to the solar plexus circle and the journey continued. I saw the tip of the spear that was the black mountain now lying in the left-hand side of my body pointing upwards. In the right-hand side, I saw exactly the same shape, but coloured yellow and pointing downwards, this spear was the Ancient Grandfather, the Power coming down. The other spear, the Grandfather of the Black Mountain, was the Power going up. Between the two spears, a brown circlular shield was suspended. It was made from the hide of the Buffalo and there was a symbol painted on it. This was a difficult moment: would I reject what I saw there?

I saw an M-shape with a long ending that was like a tail and a short beginning that was like a head. This was a symbol of the Buffalo from the spirit plains, but it looked to me remarkably like the astrological sign for Scorpio. Now, this should help me to remember it, but should not be allowed to take over and fix it in that astrological context, so it was a chunky M-shape and it was the symbol of all the browsing animals that live on the Green, particularly, in this instance, the bison itself. This symbol was painted red. It had weight. It had stability. It had strength. It had calmness. It rose up where the Power came down; it reached down where the Power rose up.

the symbol on the hide

I want the Buffalo skull to be at work and I know what the work is: it is providing help and healing. I had thought to myself: "In order to do this surely the Buffalo skull must participate in events?" And I took it to one of the Seneca seminar days, but, despite the fact that I carried an enormous wrapped bundle into the room which sat behind me all day, no-one seemed to notice it, no-one asked me what it was, and no suitable opportunity arose where it might have been a help to show it. There is no point in trying for a particular result; I have learnt this. It is something I have learnt if I ever feel I know nothing! I became content with the idea that the Buffalo hidden was as likely a way of achieving the work as the Buffalo revealed.

I offered the Buffalo skull to go on the Tree at this year's UK Sun Moon Dance and the organiser told me that the Buffalo skull at last year's Dance lived in Germany and that it would be brought over again this year by its keeper. We agreed that it would be good for the two to be at the Dance and I hoped to ask someone knowledgeable if there was anything I should do to preserve the bone. The skull stayed wrapped up and hidden in my tent and the Dance started.

On one of the Dance days, two little children, one a babe in arms, one a toddler, were brought to the Tree to be blessed by the Chief. We danced the next dance for the Children of the World. That was a very touching and beautiful moment and brought us all the blessing of innocence.

At the end of the Dance, I left the arbour and went to my tent to change my clothes. The Buffalo skull had gone. I found it in a heap with my other belongings in a damp corner of another tent. The babies had slept in my tent. This was ok, but I felt miffed that the skull had been unceremoniously moved. I found the person who had moved it and I told her that such bundles were sacred objects. She did not know this and apologised. I told her not to worry, but that I needed to point this out to her and to say that it would have been better if someone who knew about such things had moved it. A little later on I was talking this over with the keeper of the other Buffalo skull. He said to me: "Where the children are concerned there can be no wrong." I felt that my comments to the mother of the children had been out of place, and I learnt something about my own negativity there.

When the Chief learned that there was a new Buffalo skull he gave me a bundle of rawhide thongs. He told me: "Soak them in water for twenty four hours till they are pliable then bind the skull, as they dry they will shrink and hold the bone plates together tightly."

The Exam

I cannot imagine that I will get this journey down exactly right, but the spirits assured me, they assured me, when I was panicking as it got so complicated, that they would bring it to me again, again, and again until I got it. So here is my attempt.

Today I was free. There was clear space around me and the minute I came to meditate, I was there! The white Buffalo skull was in the other room, wrapped up, and it came to me. It lay upon me, big and heavy, the nose bones covered my solar plexus and my navel centre; the forehead covered my heart and throat. It entered into me until I became, completely and utterly, the white bones of the skull. This was a wonderful feeling of pure whiteness with bony simplicity and clarity and strength.

The living form of the Brown Buffalo appeared, all the growing potential of the planet, the dark fertile earth of the world, was in the body of the Buffalo and I was happy to wander there. I entered into this Buffalo and it was an entering into the spirit lodge.

I went in highly aware, highly energised, and as soon as I was in that place the colour Yellow began to spread from the centre, as it engulfed me and overwhelmed me the spirits asked me a question: "What is the colour Yellow?" I answered fairly quickly: "The colour Yellow is Be-ing. The colour Yellow is, um, everything that Be-es, everything that be-comes, everything that is."

Then the yellow was replaced with blue, and the spirits asked me very swiftly, very strongly, very abruptly: "What is the colour Blue?" I freaked out because I was still in the yellow and they were asking me a question that I felt I hardly knew the answer to. I knew I had to answer fast and not think about it. I said quickly: "The Blue is everything that flies in the sky and everything that swims in the sea. Please don't make me do this." But they did.

Then the colour Green came and they said again: "And what is the colour Green?" I answered: "The Green is everything that grows. The Green is nourishment. The Green is how the spirit grows and develops and ......" I have lost it now! I just said: "The Green is everything that grows. It nourishes everything. It is how everything grows in Be-ing."

I was then ready to go on to the next colour, which was Black, but the spirits shouted: "Stop! Stop. Stay still." I stood still in that place and into that place came purple light with emerald green. Those are the colours that I see with Joseph. Joseph came and I addressed a prayer to him: "Help me, Joseph, look, I am here, help me to learn. Oh, Beautiful Painted Arrow, please help me."

The arrow flew and embedded itself in my body. But, quite contrary to the Beautiful Painted Arrow that leaves the colours of the rainbow trailing behind it, this arrow was black. It had a triangle at the front end, a round stem, and at the back end, where the flight feathers would be, it had three horizontal bars. The longest was first on the shaft, then a shorter one, and then the shortest one behind, with a small amount of the shaft pointing out behind that.

the arrow

The head of the arrow was embedded in my psyche, in the left-hand side of my body about the level of my belly button. There was no pain with this arrow.

I thought there were to be no consequences at all, but suddenly I was looking into the open mouth of an enormous Snake and staring into the yellow tunnel of its throat. The jaws were closing round the lower part of my body and I felt the two fangs penetrate the soft part of my belly in the pelvic region; the fang that entered the left side of my body was blue and the fang that entered the right side was green. I wondered: "Am I going to suffer now and die?" Sensing the Ancient Grandfather I said: "Grandfather, Grandfather, I am dying, I am dying. I ... am ... dying." And he agreed with me.

The red tongue of the Snake flickered and the Grandfather pulled me backwards. I am getting a bit confused here, he pulled me backwards, and I think at this point the colour Black came. Yes, the colour Black, which I had expected earlier when the spirits told me to stop, came now. It poured into me and everything became Black. I knew this was the Power: the Power that came through Joseph and was coming into me. He had said: "Become the Power." And so I did that.

The beginning of the becoming was exciting, but then I didn't feel so brilliant and a little voice inside me said: "But I don't feel powerful!" I had to laugh as I realized: "Oh, you thought that becoming the Power meant that you would be powerful, did you?

Well, apparently that is not the case." And that was a salutary lesson.

Finally, everything went grey. Sometimes two levels of a metaphor run at once, and that is why it is so difficult to record the story in sequence. I think I tried to consolidate the images I had seen, and that is when the spirits assured me they would teach me this until I recalled it as it should be recorded. There were some teachings about the grey: how people are walking through a mist in the world of everyday, how everything is hidden there, how magical processes occur there, and there were some teachings about how to be a green healer within the veil of greyness by drawing healing from the colour Green.

I have been able to tell the spirits that I accept their presence, their noise, their wisdom, and their knowledge of what is coming next, and maybe there is a sort of agreement now whereby I will try to listen and they will try to tell me. But just now I am going to take myself out of this trance state, eat toast and drink tea, and maybe walk on the Fell to collect some water to soak the thongs to bind the Buffalo skull, or maybe not, because I will still be listening.

I got up, I ate toast, I drank tea, and I walked along the course of the sacred river bed. I was out for five and a half hours. It was humid and hot. The purpose of my journey was to ceremonialize the binding of the bones by getting water from the highest pool to soak the strips of hide. I had chosen to use this water partly because of the location, far up the river, and partly because it is always stained an orangey-red, perhaps from the rust of iron ore. I got to the pool, and, although the basin is seven feet deep, it was empty and bone dry. I realized that I have only once seen water in it, and that was the first time I went there. I came home. It was not the day.

The Power and I

This was a very eventful journey, which I couldn't hold together logically, so I don't quite remember how, but I was flying through the air. I came to rest on top of the Buffalo skin lodge, falling there like the skin of a buffalo covering the structure, making it dark and secret. To me, that was a wonderful thing to do, to become the skin of the buffalo and to lie upon the sacred lodge.

A spirit threw open a flap in the top of the lodge and I realized that the smoke hole is not always open; they told me it is only ever opened at night. As the flap flew open, I looked up at the night sky where silver points of light were twinkling and a spirit said joyfully: "Millions of solar lights."

I stared in amazement at the millions of suns that blazed there; how many contained planetary systems which might support life; systems that were to my sight dark, and all that I could see were the points of light around which they orbited?

I was lying belly up, my navel centre was the smoke hole and the rest of my body was the lodge. The smoke hole was wide open. I had no fear now of the tube-like extension that searches from my navel centre. Unlike the previous times when I have stared at it in horror, this time I actively encouraged and pushed my consciousness into it and I searched, I searched for the Power.

Power came in the form of a gigantic male buffalo, which filled the sky. The sky was deep blue and the buffalo was brown. I felt feminine and small and like a hole, and the buffalo bull was going to fill my navel centre. Yes, it was a sexual image of sorts and I had no inhibitions about it. I remembered the teaching Joseph gave me: "Become the Power." I opened myself and waited and the Power came in. It was clear that it was not in my psyche to deliberately try to use or abuse power; I just do not have that need any more. In fact, the only thing I knew how to do was to become the Power, and that was a finished subject, if you like, never again would I need to worry about what the Power was.

I opened up to the Power and the Power came in to dream within me in modern metaphors. I didn't hold, as I don't seem to be able to hold, the memory of these present day metaphors, but there were cookers and crumbs in the bottom of cookers, cooking pans and fast roads. It seems to me now that the Power wants me to dream in modern imagery. Well, I innately understand the ancient images, because I lived following them many times, but my modern life is very different and I do not seem to have an attachment to its metaphors. Maybe that is why this life is so confusing, and, really, maybe only the spirits understand it. So I just let the spirits formulate the Power within me while I, I suppose I enjoyed it!

Eventually I came back feeling very good, but I had lost everything. "Never mind," I thought to myself: "just get up." But I lay there for a little while longer and I found myself searching again. That is how I came to remember the beginning sections of this journey of being the skin on the lodge, of the Buffalo spirit sending power into the lodge, of the incomprehensible section about how the Power manifests in the modern world. As they came to me, I saw they were important and I decided to put them on the tape.

Autumn
The Consciousness of the Lodge

On Sunday, as I picked blackberries, a beautiful peacock butterfly was feeding on the pollen from the heads of the scabious flowers nearby and I watched it for a while, looking at the shimmering purple wings with their white painted 'eyes' and the russet red body against the bright mauve-blue flowers.

Today the Ancient Grandfather gripped me straight away, and, very soon into the meditation, this same butterfly flew and landing upon the ground that was myself closed its wings. The Grandfather came closer and, as he came so close that he was entering my head, I saw the convoluted walls of a tunnel enclosing us. This tunnel was a strange yellow colour and it felt like being inside the body of a caterpillar. Was it a snake, or an earthworm? No, it was a big fat caterpillar. This is the end of the summer and the caterpillar is pupating. The Grandfather and I are going to mix together until we are indistinguishable and then, out of this mixing, a new form is going to come.

The entering, dissolving, disappearing, mixing and moving went on. My whole mind was open and I was in no mood to reject anything, so when I perceived the Great Plains ahead of me and saw the Buffalo, I knew he was an entrance into the spirit lodge. I ducked down, under the flap of skin that is the door, and went in.

It was dark in there and I sensed I had an opportunity to feel the presence of the other spirits. At last, I was no longer too afraid, or too untutored, to be able to perceive in that place and I opened myself. It was like opening doors; opening the doors so that the holes that are perception can perceive.

Lots of spirits came to touch various parts of my Being and I felt them all. As this happened I felt a deep physical ecstasy running through me which I enjoyed, but I did not get stuck to it. I spoke to these spirits. They were a deep excitement. They were an ability to go further. They were interested in me. They welcomed me and were glad to be able to be perceived.

I hoped to see the fire that burns at the centre of the lodge. As I looked for the centre, the small area of the lodge expanded into a vast space and miles away beyond my feet, as if I was lying horizontally there, I saw the setting Sun. Our Sun was the fire at the centre of the lodge. I saw the whole of the, um, the, um, oh dear, the words are hard. I saw the lodge as the consciousness of the Earth. I saw that the Earth circles the Sun, but that the Earth consciousness actually encircles the Sun, so that, although at that moment I was in one place, it could be possible to have that whole orbit of awareness within my consciousness, and for a second I saw it, so I must have had it. This was a deeply extraordinary and moving vision of the fire in the centre and I knew the spirits of the lodge had brought it to me. I was full of gratitude and I certainly thanked them.

Then there is a blank patch. I am sure a great pulse of blue light came, followed by black, followed by yellow. Then I feel I was drifting when I saw something questing in the darkness. I immediately knew that something was looking for me, in fact, I knew that it was a Being from another dimension, and I was willing for this Being to find me. I stretched my navel centre towards it and there was a joining there.

I felt no fear and I did not feel any excitement either, I just felt, this is happening and this is good, and I put my open centre to the awareness of the other Being and I saw it: silver with black eyes. This Being came to me and it walked in my consciousness, not like the Grandfather who now was metamorphosing with me, no, this Being walked, and I watched it walk, through my body. I called it a Being of Peace.

I came back from that place because the top of my scalp began to itch and I came back to scratch that itch. Yes, I came back to put this on the tape. That Being is tall with limbs that are thin and tubular, with eyes that are black and teardrop-shaped. Oh, it didn't say much to me, or indeed, anything. That alien is from another dimension, um, I can't say any more than that, but because I feel so strongly that it is peaceful I am happy to welcome it. I am sure I said: "Welcome." And, while we were together, there was a perception of the great net, the holes of which are more important than their boundaries. I heard that some of the holes are red and some of the holes are blue, and it is through these red and blue holes that the Peace Beings come.

Winter

Give Up the Drug

When I began to meditate this morning, I called out to and concentrated upon the Buffalo. The Buffalo skull and the living spirit Buffalo were there. Slowly the Buffalo grew in size and in intensity and I was on the Great Plains. I looked for the spirit lodge, and when I came to it the spirits laid me down on a stretcher in order to take me in feet first, but I was far too big and I realized that, at the size I was, I could not get in. I thought about it for a while and reached the conclusion that the only way I would be able to enter was as an earthworm. I became a little, legless, pink and vulnerable earthworm and wriggled into the lodge like that. Once in I coiled myself up and looked around.

The two Grandfathers came and I had a choice to go with one or the other. I chose to go with the Ancient Grandfather. There followed a moment when there were many hypodermics about and, by this metaphor, he suggested to me that I cease to take the adrenaline shots that I have previously depended on to run my life, that I cease to fuel the forward motion of my life by setting and meeting deadlines. A deadline is like the jolt of a drug injection because the end time by which something has to be done is fast arriving, and that is like depending upon heroin for my motivation. So he would like me to give up that mode of being, and I will try and think hard about how to do that.

The Fire Ceremony

Yesterday was the seventh day of the month, fire ceremony day, a ceremony given by Oceanus to Joseph, Beautiful Painted Arrow, in a vision. Through this ceremony the Oceans of the mind, the world and the cosmos, are cleansed by the lighting of a ceremonial fire.

At two o'clock, I left the house knowing that it would be dark about four. It had been raining heavily for several days but the morning was dry and the weather was warm. I put on all my rain kit and drove up to the Fell. Although the river bed is usually dry, I had the feeling that there could be water in the top pool. As I drove along the high road and looked down into the valley, I saw that even the bed of the river was glistening with the silver light reflected off water, this was pretty exciting. I parked the car and started to walk. The ground was waterlogged, soft and squelchy, very beautiful to walk on, but the rain would come in squalls and I would hide inside my clothes and soak up the atmosphere without looking around.

I walked the few miles to the highest pool. A large volume of water was pouring into it and it was nearly full to the brim. I chose a place to lay the fire, right in front of the entrance to the pothole that is on the edge of that pool. I laid the maize and the tobacco circles, ensuring that the Ancestors would be present. It was a new pouch of tobacco and the smell, enhanced by the mossy dampness of the

Fell, was glorious. Inside the circles, I laid twenty-eight sticks in a square stack, put some combustible material in the centre and lit the fire. I prayed to the Mother in the earth, the dark Mother-of-lost-beginnings. I prayed for her to forgive us and have mercy on us. It came to me again how arrogant it is to assume that we can kill the Earth and that we can heal it too. I prayed for her to heal us and not to toss us off the planet for being destructive pests.

The fire-stack was burning beautifully; it was a magnificent place to be watching the fire, with its dancing red light, burning brightly against the backdrop of grey limestone. In front of it, the silver-grey water of the pool reflecting and transforming the deep grey of the lowering clouds above. Behind it, the dark entrance to the cave system, a vertical crack in the rock, just a slit, which a grown person would need to crouch down in front of and squeeze through to get in. Beyond the entrance, the internal walls of the cave glistening in the firelight like the eyes of snakes. The low waterfall dropping the rushing water into the basin, causing the water to make wonderful musical notes, and below that the occasional deep boom as a rock shifted in the bottom of the pool.

The wind, not cold, blowing and invigorating my lungs. It was easy to praise the elements there and to sing and that is what I did. When the fire had died down, I collected enough of the rusty-coloured water from the pool to soak and soften the leather thongs for binding together the plates of the Buffalo skull.

Dark Waters

Today a van full of my belongings goes to Scotland. I slept in the study last night because my bedroom is disassembled. I played my drum for a while and I was in a restless state when I first went to bed. I tried to meditate, the Buffalo skull came and filled the room but I fell away from this healing power and got stuck in pain. I decided to try to sleep, and I asked the spirits to wake me if they would teach me. Later on I did wake up and there was an incomprehensible process, which I entered into and tried to remember but I cannot speak about it because it does not lend itself to being talked of in any terms of reference that I know from our world of everyday.

This morning the White Buffalo came to my left. I was overcome by the whiteness and, lying down, I became the ground. A few little green shoots had pushed their way through the chalk surface of this white ground, only a very, very few green shoots on such sterile growing ground, and certainly not enough to feed the Buffalo. Beside the Buffalo, I saw a tall green Maize plant growing, heavy with cobs of yellow corn.

My navel centre held a pool of inky black water. Would the Buffalo and the Maize plant drink this water? Yes, the Buffalo put her purple tongue to the water, and the roots of the Maize plant found the water there, but where was 'there'? Did the surface of the pool catch the sun's light and reflect the blue sky or, perhaps, the landscape? No, in the black waters there were no reflections. Something was amiss and I tried to puzzle it out. If there was no reflection then the process motivated by the engine of the Sun, the cycle of evaporation of the water on the surface of the planet rising up into the sky and falling again as rain, was not the cycle that sustained the White Buffalo spirit and the Yellow Corn Mother. There must be another source of water sustaining them.

Where was the water that was black and dark and still, and not involved in the cyclic process? The answer was deep inside the Earth in the prehistoric water reservoirs. I travelled into the earth to this deep level of ancient planetary water. It was a no-happening place and I questioned my purpose in coming there. It led me to wondering what the effect would be of drawing this water out of the earth and turning it into water that became part of the evaporation process. What kind of ecological consequences would be caused? But this was human thought and anxiety. I returned my attention to the dark reservoirs and simply waited.

I began to perceive blue light: "Oh, this is the nourishment of the spirit Beings." I saw that the Buffalo spirit and the Maize spirit draw upon the blue light hidden in the ancient water and I became that blue light. That was perfection as far as I was concerned.

Entering the Black Buffalo

Maybe I was a little too optimistic at the beginning of this journey. I had the idea that if I pushed to make something happen, it would happen, and that is how I set off, but everything I tried to do, everything I tried to move, and every time I tried to travel, nothing happened.

I began to be of the opinion that, by the intrusion of my desires, I was going to be going absolutely nowhere. I let go a bit and I began to travel in the darkness, travelling through a night sky full of silver light, going back to the experience the previous night of seeing the aurora borealis, and travelling onwards. Seeing and travelling into a black pyramid and beginning to consider the impression I have of an ancient life spent in a cool, dark temple. I accepted the darkness, accepted the movement, and began to travel through a series of ancient buildings, one of which had silver light entering through a hole in the ceiling. But nothing happened in these places and I continued to travel on.

I had become quite resigned to the fact that I would simply travel in the darkness, seeing the occasional temple and sanctuary, till the end of the journey, when I saw ahead of me the head of the Black Buffalo. I said: "I know you! I have seen you before." I moved towards it. When I had first seen the Black Buffalo, it was tiny, dense, invertedly energetic; its whole body so tightly curled up on itself that it was condensed into a dark ball the size of a postage stamp. Now only the head was hanging there in the black space, much larger than myself. I travelled slowly towards it, observing the curly, metallically coloured black coat, the very broad, flat forehead and the wide spreading horns. In the very centre of the forehead was a golden hole from which issued forth golden light. I put my solar plexus to that golden hole. The image was graphic. The sensation was powerful. Through that hole I went, into the space that is within that Black Buffalo Being.

the black buffalo

A surprise awaited me. It was a very peculiar place in there. It was dark, but it was not black, the space was fizzing with whiteness. I felt my awareness of my shape change. I began to lose my body contours and to become, I presumed, the shape of the Buffalo, but it was a round contour-less shape that I became and after that absolutely nothing changed. There was a feeling of intense density and pressure and I only had my awareness left. I had nothing else; the awareness of being fizzing dark matter filled my consciousness. The sensation was not painful, it was not threatening. It was ....., I'd like to use the word 'ghastly'. It was a very difficult place to be in because there was nothing to be experienced there except density and pressure.

I searched through my experience for something similar. The only thing it reminded me of was when I was a child, sometimes when I lay in bed at night, my head used to feel very huge. The childhood sensation that went with that was like crunching cotton wool in your hand, but the sensation on this journey was like a pressing weight, an immobile pushing-ness, a kind of suffocation. It did not take my breath; I seemed not to breathe. I distinctly did not like being in there, and, although the sensation was extraordinary and I was certainly questioning what on earth kind of a place it was, I would have very much liked to get out of it, but I couldn't see how that was possible. I seemed to have lost my body and to have lost the ability to move. I noticed that panic was an option, and I determined to stay calm.

Into the darkness, I called very quietly: "Grandfather?" hoping that he would hear and help me. When I called the pressure and the sensation that was so strange began to diminish at once, and the strange darkness began to become pure black light. With relief, I knew that the Ancient Grandfather would take me out of there, but, as I felt the place diminish, I became aware that somehow this outcome was disappointing. The Grandfather would never make me suffer when I could not stand it, but I felt a sense of defeat in coming out and I chose to go back.

I went back. It was exactly as it had been, and it became very clear to me that I had to surrender in that place because there was nowhere else to go and nothing else to do. I did surrender and something broke inside me. Something around the level of my solar plexus seemed to be laid upon a block there and broken in half, like a piece of brittle metal. It snapped and tears rolled out of my eyes. It was a terrible moment because that was the end: that was it.

Very shortly after this catastrophic self-sacrificial moment for nothing, that strange state began to diminish and I came back to my body lying flat on its back in the seminar room. Tears were falling out of my eyes and running into my ears. I lay looking at the shadow of the centre light on the ceiling. Due to the candle, burning on the medicine altar directly underneath, there was a black shadow cast on the ceiling with a white centre and another black circle in the centre of that. These shadows made the shape of an eye. I looked at it for a long time wondering if it would take me on another journey, but it did not, and, quite frankly, I was happy to just be back lying there in a familiar room.

I don't know what the crushing breaking place was, or why I needed to go there. All I know is that the Ancient Grandfather would have taken me out of that state had I persisted in my request, and this proves to me that nothing is done by compulsion in the spirit world. It is all done by choice, and it is very possible that I made the right choice there, to go back, and that pleased the Grandfather. But he would not have been displeased with me if I had come out; I would have been displeased with myself.

Spring

The Fall

    This morning I followed the Power through a lot of images that I observed and let go. At one point, the Maize Mother was close and I saw many green geometric shapes each composed of two lines making a right angle between them, things I couldn't understand. I was looking at something else, which I couldn't understand, to do with Maize, when there was a funny little click noise and, in a quick flash, I saw the colours green and blue moving together. Hum, the meditation lasted an hour. When it was over I felt surprisingly relaxed, I felt myself enter a deeply quiet, calm, and thoughtless place. I disappeared there.

    I was lifting the Buffalo skull up from the end of the bed when the lower jaw fell off. Never mind that it doesn't have a lower jaw, the jaw fell off and struck the floor. I laid the skull down on the bed again, picked up the jawbone and examined it for damage. As I bent forward to put it back beneath the top jaw, I began to fall into the skull. I was fully aware of the everyday world where I lay on the bed in a trance and at the same time, I was experiencing this exciting opportunity to jump into the white skull of the Buffalo. The fall was not initiated by me, but it was happening to me. Poised there I threw myself into the experience, shouting out in affirmative joy: "T-ah!" My voice made no sound in the everyday world, but it sounded very loudly in this other place. I fell and fell through the vast expanse, hearing, with my everyday ears, the tremendous noise of air rushing past me. It was not like the fluctuating sound of the wind but a consistent roar. I listened to the sound of falling and did not resist in any way.

In my visionary forehead, I saw the Buffalo formed in shimmering light, light that was blue with green and yellow in it. The light image was of the Buffalo running, except that it was still. I could see the four legs in running position, the head with horns carried low at the front, the shoulder muscles bunched, the bulk of the body behind, the tail held high: an electric image, which became stronger.

I was able to look and look, and I was focused on maintaining the experience. I am certain there was nothing in me that was afraid, or that was questioning the reality, or whether it was dangerous, or the right thing to do. There was no question of doubt and yet this state began to diminish and just disappeared.

I lay here on my bed, a pain in my solar plexus, not unpleasant, and the Buffalo was filling the room. Although the intensity of the visionary experience was gone, I stayed with the feeling of it for as long as I could. I don't know what more there is to say, and so I won't say any more.

Summer

The Mycelium

I began my meditation journey this morning calling out: "Father!" I called out again, cautiously: "Father?" and, feeling immediately aware in my spirit body, I travelled in the darkness. I travelled towards a Red diamond. As my body opened up and I felt my awareness increasing, the diamond went Blue. I travelled towards it still. What is the diamond shape? It is the symbol of the Father, who is also the Mother. Eventually, having no thoughts only visions, I discovered that I had become acutely aware in my spirit body; right up to the top of my head I could feel myself moving and expanding into a greater space than I normally occupy. I began to see Joseph, Joseph who is the Father-Mother walking in the world of everyday, a medicine person and a Teacher.

Joseph became a black oval and I travelled through him into a deep cave. This cave was like a lecture theatre and ranks of many Beings were already there. They were crouching down with bent heads. At first, I thought they were wearing hats because they all had a groove along the top of their heads, which looked like the soft fold of a grey fedora. I was floating over the top of this mass of people and, viewed from above, the sight reminded me of a large group of fungi.

Realizing that I had been able to come there through Joseph I prayed for help to understand what was happening. Soon it seemed to me that I should join this group, but they were very densely packed upon the ground of that place and I felt a reluctance in myself to become part of this peculiar organism. Nevertheless, I allowed myself to drift and look, and eventually I did find a small spot where I could land and become a member of this mycelium.

I felt myself become different and I was no longer alone. I was part of this network of strange Beings and as I became attached there, I discovered myself to be bending over too. My eyes were looking into my belly button and they became part of that lower body awareness. Previously, my head had been sticking up above the crowd and I did not feel any different to my normal self, but when my eyes, my belly button, and my solar plexus, all focused in the same place, which was below the level of the top of this group of Beings, then I became the same as them.

After this had happened, Joseph changed colour and he became a colour that does not exist in the daily world, a silver-gold no-colour. I suppose that we were all like that, and every

Being in that place was concentrating inwards in a way that made all the divisions in their own person disappear and helped them to become part of this one Being that was concentrating on achieving something.

As I rooted myself down there, I realized that the mycelium was the world I live in. The inward looking-ness that I experienced in among that great group was from spirit people whose awareness was concentrating in this world. It was in this world of everyday that something was trying to be achieved, although I still do not know exactly what that is. It was a very surprising moment to see that mycelium as a metaphor of existence in our world and it gave me a whole new insight on the nature of my life.

The Buffalo skull, which I have partly unwrapped ready to go to the third UK Sun Moon Dance, came to me in that place as the brown living Buffalo. Then I saw the four forms of the Buffalo: the Brown, the Black, which I saw with a bit of a fright because I did not want to be drawn to travel in there, the White, and the Blue. In realms of Greatness, these are the colours of the spiritual spaces of the Buffalo.

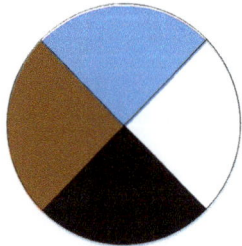

buffalo colour wheel

It was the Brown that called me. As I moved towards it, I went to the time when it was just a few hunters and the bison. We killed the great beast, stabbed it with spears until it died; a most dangerous way of doing, but the only way open to us, only through the death of the bison would we live. When the bison lay dead on the ground, there in front of me was the metaphor of abundance diminished by my needs. That was the way it was and we hunters knew that expressing love, respect and gratitude to the Being that sustained us ensured the continuance of life.

I moved from there to my life now and I found myself within the oval of a building, a Peace Chamber, which had the same feeling as the body of the Buffalo. The last image I remember was of standing between the legs of the Buffalo encompassed by its huge bulk. This planted in me the idea that building a Chamber was the way I could express gratitude to the Being that sustains me.

Draw On the Abundance

We danced our third Sun Moon Dance in the UK. During the ceremony, the Chief called a dreaming dance, instructing the dancers to lie down and dream while the drum played a fast rhythm. During this time, I saw enormous numbers of animals. I saw a herd of buffalo, millions strong, then thousands of migrating caribou, next a herd of wildebeest, numberless, and what was the last herd? That was what the spirits left for me to find out: it was an immense shoal of fish.

The poignancy of this dream was that the buffalo had already gone, and how soon would the others follow? Among the possible things that I saw in the future during the dreaming time was a world where such numbers of animals no longer existed, and I saw what that meant for the psyche of the children, how it would be for the children of that time when the diversity of animal life no longer remained. It was quite clear that life would continue, but for someone who had had a taste of those natural bounties of animals this was a sad vision. The shamanic people of the future driving in their cars would see empty but brightly coloured crisp packets blowing along the edges of the roads and, seeking inspiration, would chase them in their dreaming.

Yesterday it was a long slow drive back from the Dance site home to Scotland with a big heavy load in the trailer, but it wasn't stressful and I found a cheap place to eat with food that was straightforward and good, so I felt blessed.

When I reached my new home, I hung the Buffalo skull, which had recently hung on the Sun Moon Dance Tree, above the fireplace. It looked beautiful, the Power of the Sun Moon Dance was resting in it, radiating from it, and all the memories of the Power brought the Power to life right there. It seemed too great a blessing for me to sit there on my own with the Buffalo, so I prayed that the energy of the Dance would nourish everybody who was there and that their lives would become rich and their awareness would continue to expand for as long as the beautiful Buffalo held the Power like a storage radiator.

The Silver Cords

I entered the travelling trance this morning and I saw the ancient standing stone monument of Callinish, on the Island of Lewis in Scotland, a place I had visited after the Dance with an american friend. In the largest stone I saw the gateway to other worlds through which silver light shines, an entrance not visible in the light of everyday but accessible in the meditative world. I went towards it but as I was about to go through, the terrible difficulties caused by people's needs diverted me, pulled my attention away from the hole, and I became utterly involved in the human dynamic of my daily life.

After wending my way through this labyrinth for some time, becoming more and more distressed about what choices to make, I noticed that my heart was not beating correctly. This had been true as I woke up, and now again it came to my attention that there was an erratic beat in my heart. Why, at other times when I am travelling or intensely working and connected to the dreaming world, why does my heart not fail me then under that intense effort, whereas something like this on a human level upsets me so much?

I recalled the gift of the peaceful heart that was offered to me by the spirits as I participated in a Sun Moon Dance in Australia and I knew that I must do something to activate that gift. I called for help and the spirits advised: "Draw on the abundance of the Buffalo." I pulled myself through the darkness of the labyrinth and, feeling something solid in the darkness, grasped hold of a horn. I had found him. A strange beast because there was the skull hanging on the front room wall but behind it there was an invisible Buffalo body that was like a huge bed or platform. I laid myself there, feeling immediately better.

Slowly I began to sink through the platform into the now visible body of the Buffalo. The brown hide encased me and I felt the living beauty of the Brown, the place of safety where Peace could be. The spirit lodge of the Buffalo surrounded me and I looked at a scene I have looked at before where there is a floor of brown earth and a ceiling of brown buffalo hide and between them a thin horizontal space that is full of emptiness. I was happy to be there and to know that I had returned to a place with which I am familiar and which is a place of learning.

The silver disc of the Moon, radiant with pale moonbeams, was shining down upon me. The Moon is the portal, the open hole in the big stone at Callinish. I still don't understand the strong connection between the Buffalo and the Moon, but there, it is so! Looking at the silver hole, I heard a brisk voice say: "Time for some radical action." A brief moment for silent reflection followed. Then, spoken in a matter-of-fact tone, I heard: "No time like the present." It meant: "This is the best time to do it." But then 'no time like the present' changed its meaning and it meant: "No time, just like the present has no time." I was confused. I struggled and struggled to remember Joseph's phrase about Time in the present. I found it: 'the timeless moment'. Ah, if only I could live there!

There was no time like the present and it was time for radical action. The radical action was to go through that hole, not be held back by daily concerns, but to go through. I went through into the extraordinary silver light, light that is created by the Sun, and yet, I don't know, being a reflection does it allow awareness without destruction? I don't know, but I went through into the presence of the Silver Spirits. Their name is Wah-ch-ken-ay, Beings who plant the Breath of Beauty from the heavenly plains. Those spirits do not come to the Earth: that I know. They are catalysts of life here, but they do not allow themselves to be changed and they do not come here. It is necessary to go there.

Blackness formed the backdrop to the silver lights, and I saw the mysterious vision of rushing points of silver light against black space that I see occasionally during a Sun Moon Dance. This image was before me now, and with it there came a complete change to my perception of the Black Buffalo, I was no longer wary.

I saw the image of a silver cord. When the silver cord is broken, I have often heard tell, it is the ending of an individual life. Now I saw a silver cord, and I also saw more silver cords stretching downwards in the black space, taut, holding me in place. I looked up to where the Silver Spirits were and I knew that a prayer cut the silver cords: "Please, oh Spirits of the Silver Light cut the cords." Well, that was one of those moments, where a part of me was completely shocked by what I was saying and another part was completely sure that this was what I wanted to say.

The Spirits took silver scissors and began to cut those cords. The first one went with a tremendous bang. As it shot away, I saw a disappearing point of silver light and I thought: "That's the vision from the Sun Moon Dance, the cords snapping, the cords being broken, the cords being cut. How many are there to each individual body?" and the Silver Spirits cut four cords.

The last one was the only one that caused me any pain, on the left-hand side of my neck, internally. I am sure that is the cord which is causing my heart palpitations, and they cut that one last. I dwelt for a while in the feelings that the cutting of that final cord had given me: the feelings in my heart as it left me, and the feelings of watching it disappear. It seemed to me that in the breaking of that cord was the secret of the peaceful heart.

Now I was in suspension somewhere in the blackness; the cords that had attached me downwards were gone. I wondered what was next. I turned my consciousness over and it seemed a good idea to take the stumps, which were left on my body, and send them in a different direction, upwards.

The first emanated from the right-hand side of my body, towards the centre line above my right breast, it flew up and struck something silver. The second one, from below the right breast but also towards the centre and on the front of the rib cage, fired and hit blue. The next one, about the level of the solar plexus, fired and hit green. The last one, from lower down, hit yellow.

I saw the smooth and silver belly of something above me. Hum, what was it? It was the Mother ship. I was like a small ship attached by four struts of light to the underbelly of a gigantic Mother ship. What was this strange alien image created by the Beings of the Silver Light in the place through the porthole of the Moon? I was hanging in a vast ocean attached to the belly of an enormous Dolphin. The Dolphin was the Mother ship and I was attached to the silver-ness there. All the problems caused by the dynamics of needy people had gone. I felt happy.

It was time to return and to try again to hold myself in detachment. Try again to have no hidden agendas and to have no .... erm ..., oh, that's good because I have forgotten the word, so obviously I haven't got any of it! Um, what is the word? I think the word must be 'wants', but it seems to be rather a short word. I thought it was a much longer word with at least three syllables and very, very heavy, um, about the things that .... ah! .... 'expectations' that's the word! And I had NO expectations out there with the Silver Beings once they had decided there was no time like the present. I would love, love, love to live my life like that.

The Ancient Ones

I went on a visit to my relations, I mean my human relations this time. For our various reasons, in the evening, we were all very tired and we went to bed early. But no sleep for me; I became involved in a very physical and challenging process which was hurting me a lot and causing me to be very restless in my mind. I suddenly burst through into a space of complete tranquillity. What a relife (oops, a mistype for 'relief'), there I was lying in my spirit body in a peaceful place.

That very afternoon access to the peaceful heart had been established in my everyday world by a bison bull in the Wildlife Park near Aviemore that I visited on the way to my brother's house. It happened that, because of the foot and mouth outbreak, cars could not be driven into the Park and we were taken round in a special bus instead. The small herd of Wisent, the european bison, thirteen strong, were browsing near the track and the driver stopped the bus. He opened the door and I sat on the step taking photographs. The old bull left the cow that he was interested in, and walked to the door of the bus to look intently at me. Behind me, the bus driver whispered: "The emergency exit is at the back!" but that was of no interest to me whatsoever because I was completely absorbed in the aura of that magnificent animal. After he had posed for his photograph for a few minutes, he returned to the cow. That experience deeply inspired me and helped me through the barriers.

Resting in the peaceful place, I discovered myself to be standing exactly at the centre of my Being and to be with Joseph. Joseph was going to introduce me to a Grandfather. I noticed that my awareness of what was behind me was opening up and that I was looking into a room that is usually hidden.

A Grandfather was there, a small, not excessively small but certainly smaller than average, old man of intense roundness and smoothness and quiet safety. I knew him very well, but the new Grandfather, who came towards me with arms that stretched out to enfold me, was strange and amorphous; most like a spaghetti spoon in shape and black, or like a leech or a sea slug, or those small flat worms that live in ponds and can radically change their shape. Arms came round to embrace me and I struggled in myself with this completely incomprehensible Being, accepting the fact that all of these experiences are in effect incomprehensible and that, having been seen, the struggle of the metaphoric mind is to bring them into images that have some meaning in daily life while still resonating back to the original. So there was this Black Being stretching out to embrace, and also, I noticed, a White Being looking vaguely as if it had horns.

the most ancient ones

After a while, I heard that these are the spirits in the hidden room and that they are the most Ancient Ones. I recalled the process when the Buffalo had taken me back, back, back in Time, thousands of years, and shown me how the life of human Beings was connected with and sustained by the bison. It seemed to me that these spirits of the hidden room, the Ancient Ones, came from even further back, and that, constantly changing their form, they have carried life to this time and place, and the process is ancient, so ancient it is nearly beyond thinking. Eh-wh....! That is how long life has lived on life.

Autumn

A Song to the Buffalo

The beginning of my meditation this morning is missing, but eventually I reached a wall of heat and physical discomfort and I wanted to get through. While I was busy fighting with myself and believing that I probably would not make it, suddenly I was through the other side. Far away in the distance, I saw a White Buffalo and

I knew from this sight that I had broken through a barrier into the spirit plains.

I sang to call the Buffalo as I have been doing in recent days. The tune is always spontaneous and the first song I had sung to the Buffalo had only one word. It was: "Buffalo....., Buffalo .....," a calling song. Then yesterday another word came, and I sang: "Buffalo walk. Buffalo walk." Today I sang: "Buffalo walk in. Buffalo walk in." After singing this invitation, I heard: "Buffalo walk in Beauty." The way this song developed was so simple, so beautiful, and so surprising.

The White Buffalo moved towards me. I was diverted for a moment by my daily life and when I looked again she had walked on past. I turned round in order to follow but I saw that she was falling to the ground. Soon only the skin of the Buffalo was lying there with a bump in the centre; a bump that might be a person concealed underneath masquerading as a buffalo to get near to the herd. This puzzled me extremely: "Why hide under a white buffalo robe which will surely attract their attention?" The impulse overtook me to crawl under that white skin and be with whoever was under there. I dived underneath that robe. It was the Buffalo skin lodge and today the skin covering the lodge was white.

I turned my body upwards and touched the lodge skin with my energy centres. The feeling did not stay in my navel centre. It moved to my heart and up to my head. I was overcome by the Great Spirit of Femininity and I became a woman in the beauty of the White Buffalo. I noticed another woman there, one that I do not like. I struggled and came to terms with her appearance there. I saw another woman there, one that I admire. Then I knew that all women had within them a part of the White Buffalo and that was part of their highest potential.

Winter

Out Of Darkness Came Light

Yesterday I finished writing the story of this year's UK Sun Moon Dance. Last night, late, I drew the picture for the front cover. Travelling in meditation this morning I saw those two guardian Beings at the top of the Tree, staring steadfastly towards the East gate and protecting the arbour from intruders, behind them, the Buffalo looking to the West.

sun moon dance tree

In the West, within the circle of the arbour, I noticed a square opening. The space within was a chaos of deep black and vibrant yellow, and I knew it was the entrance to the Thunder Eagle. When looking at the Thunder Eagle I find that I must not try to see a fixed form, but I must look at the mystical, incomprehensible, formlessness of it, which is distinguishable by the fact that it is the Black and the Yellow Lights mixing and moving together in one Being.

I decide to walk through the square opening, but I did not want to go alone. I backed up towards the Tree, feeling the Tree strong against my spine, and, above me, the head of the Buffalo, hanging there, staring into the void. I sent my attention up to the Buffalo skull. The love and the power of the skull poured down into my body. I felt that any moment, I could rise and be taken away in the ecstasy of the Buffalo spirit, but I kept my feet upon the ground and did not allow my attention to wander from the swirling yellow and black vortex in the square hole.

I invited the Buffalo and the Sun Moon Dance Tree to enter the vortex with me and the three of us went forward into the turbulence of the yellow and black lights. The Buffalo skull assumed the form of the Black Buffalo, and, inside the domain of the Thunder Being, this Buffalo could walk. He walked behind me and, when I was unable to move, pushed me forward gently, powerfully, inexorably.

I was carrying the Sun Moon Dance Tree on my back and I thought: "The Buffalo is helping me and knows what I need. What about the Tree?" I could make a crutch out of it, a stick that would help me propel myself along, or I could light it and use it as a torch so that I could see because the place we had entered was pitch dark. But I was content to be and to be moving in that place without light. And I did not want to use the Sun Moon Dance Tree as a crutch; as if it was something that was merely there to support me.

I stopped thinking about what I might do and, returning my attention to the present moment, I found that the Tree and I were leaning at an angle of about forty-five degrees to the horizontal. We were halfway between lying down and standing up and we were becoming one. I raised my arms up so that they mirrored the Y-shape of the Tree, my head dropped forward to become the Buffalo skull. The Black Buffalo, now only a skin, lay over us and formed the third layer of this sacrifice, my self below, the Tree in the centre, and the Buffalo surrounding us, but all of us one. My arms were the arms of the fork of the Tree; my head, the head of the Buffalo; my spine, the trunk of the Tree; my skin, the skin of the Buffalo.

In this way, we travelled on, looking at the two lights of the Thunder Being and hearing that the black light of the Thunder Eagle is the creator of the yellow light. It is the great magical secret power and mystery of the Thunder Being that out of the Darkness came Light. I don't think anybody could understand or control this mystery, and that is the Greatness of the Thunder Eagle.

The Abundance of Our Planet

I saw Joseph standing there and I thanked him, I thanked him for his dispassion. That was my word for his passionate detachment, which is the greatest help. I now know that seeing Joseph means that I will be able to see something in the dark space and I looked.

At a far, far distance, I saw three bell shapes: a green one to the left, a blue one in the centre, a white one to the right.

distant bells

I travelled towards them not trying to make them anything but knowing that they were becoming, and I saw a group of tall, thin Buffalo spirits standing there: one blue, one white, and one green.

buffalo spirits

This was a puzzle for me to solve. The Thunder Eagle's essence was to my right and that made me very aware that this was a vision given to me by the Thunder Being, and as I looked at the three colours I knew: "Sky, Water, and Green." The Buffalo began to mill together and I saw the planet there in the darkness, a marvellous swirling mixture of Blue and White and Green.

"Is the sky blue? Is the water blue? Neither, they are both essentially transparent, so where does the colour Blue come from?" That was the thought that came to me and I could not answer it. I opted for blue above, and the question then was: "If the sky is perceived as the colour Blue how come the water is symbolized by the colour White?"

My question was answered by a vision: the White is the water held in cloud-form and snow-form, the Green is life sustaining life, and the Blue is the colour of the all-embracing sky, which when reflected off the mirror-surface of the liquid form of water causes the Ocean to appear to be blue, making the Above accessible Below. This is a vision of the abundance of our World, especially created as a place for our consciousnesses to be, to see, to feel and to hear: to be here.

sky, water, green

A New Beginning

The Gift of the Green

Today the Ancient Grandfather came to visit me. We established contact and he told me that I am one of his hollow bones. We travelled out over the void where he showed me how it was possible for the drumstick, the hollow bone that was my body, to hit the surface of the drum, which was the surface of the void, and the vibrations that were set up here and there, would bring changes to the world. But I was the drumstick and not the drummer; that is what I felt from looking at this vision.

Then I saw an old Buffalo sitting on the plains. This Buffalo was dying. I approached quietly to give a blessing and to say thank you. Later on in my journey, I had a strong and delicate contact with a new Buffalo, which emerged fully formed out of the Green.

While I was entering into a union with this new Buffalo the need, the fear and the longing, which much of my life had been filled with until now, came before me. The task of the day, if you like, was to drop this way of being. And, actually, with relief, I let it go, knew that it was over, knew that I could open my awareness to something that would be incoming; a new way of being that would be beyond fear and personal need. This is what the new Buffalo is bringing, and with it comes the message:

"Human Beings are the Abundance now."

Abouts

About the Ancestors

I was always aware of my family ancestors but never paid much attention to my mother's stories about them; something I regretted later on when, after my mother died, I noticed that an important element in making changes to my life was to revisit the emotional and social legacies from their lives that lived on in me.

I looked into our family history and, travelling back through the generations, I came to the industrial revolution. In the turmoil of that radical transformation, I realized that the ancestors had done all they could to leave a better life for their descendants. I was, and still am, full of gratitude for their intent. Could there be a greater gift?

During that work, my concept of Ancestors began to expand, particularly when, helped by my Teachers, I began to participate in chanting and ceremony. It seemed appropriate to give thanks and to address prayers to those who had gone before, and it was not long before the Ancestors that live within me, that live in my DNA, began to reply.

Sometimes they look through my eyes and listen with my ears to the sights and sounds of the modern world, to see if they recognise anything. Sometimes they sing through me, telling stories of ceremonies long gone by. Once, while I was chanting, the rocks deep in the earth, below the chamber I was in, showed me that they remembered a time when there was NO SUN!

I am made of Ancestors; my lineage, and that of every other human Being, extends way, way back, to the dawn of Time. Back to where I am able to call the Earth 'Mother' in the same way that I once called my own mother. So everything that enabled me to be here is my Ancestor and everything that is here with me is a Relative. Learning that from every cell in my body, I determined to treat them with more respect than I had done previously by listening to what they have to say.

A short while after the four years in this book, following Joseph's vision, I built a chamber where people chant together to find the way to world peace; I built a Sound Peace Chamber, a place made of Ancestors, a place where Ancestors congregate, a place where it is possible to sing oneself into harmony.

About Language

Composed of vibration, sound has no physical form. It has been formed; in spoken language, for example, by lungs, larynx and mouth; but in itself sound is formless and can only be held formlessly, in memory. It is not surprising that more than one mystical tradition and the scientific theory of the 'Big Bang' place sound at the beginning of creation.

Originally, language was a cascading stream of sound, and words were not individualised in the way that they are now, but something happened to language when writing was invented; it stopped being formless. Words were separated out, given a form, and, placed on a flat surface, got stuck in two dimensions. In this way, writing caused words to stand still, whereas speech flows.

Spoken language is a matter for the ears and written language for the eyes; in people who are literate, the eyes have it! Ask a person who can read English which of the primal vowels sounds are in the name 'Michael', they will likely say '-ii -ah -eh', but those are not the sounds they hear; they are the letters they see. This indicates that people-who-read tend to 'see', rather than to 'hear', words. Even when the words are spoken, seeing the form often takes precedence over hearing the vibration.

Being a person who was educated to 'see' words above 'hearing' them, I chant to address the balance. Chanting enlivens listening and so returns a word to a stream of sound. Hidden levels of inspiration emerge in the resonance, reinvigorating the dormant metaphors of modern language. My perception of the word expands from a few black marks on a white page to a multi-coloured work of art, transforming a definition into infinite possibility.

I love to explore the relationship between words as forms and words as vibrations, trying to reconnect with the ancient potency of sound to awaken awareness and bringing that awareness to the analytical precision of the modern world. I do this to discover who I am and why I might be here.

About Guidance

In dreams, there is often a companion or a guide; that detail does not cause any scepticism because a dream is deemed to be an unconscious experience. In other forms of altered state work, the experience is more conscious and this is what opens the results up to question. Even though my worldview had tottered and I had chosen to look for help in less familiar places, my modern sceptical attitude gave me nothing but problems.

At the beginning of my inner space search, I experienced pain, unnerving sensations, and interruptions from persistent thoughts. After a while these ceased and deep, dark, comforting blackness arrived. Then a different type of experience began, from the darkness and the silence came hints of something other; I had asked for help and that is the beginning of help.

Yes, surely, help would involve guidance but at the first hint of 'otherness', my everyday mind fought the idea of spirit guides. I could not blame it for trying to keep me in the 'safe' place but I tried to suspend its judgements and, in learning how to do that, my transit from daily life consciousness to inner space became easier. Nowadays, I check the validity of my experiences not by asking: "Is it real?" but by asking: "Is it helpful?"

For a while, I did hope that I might one day be with the guides in eternity, but now I think that is not likely when I no longer have a body. Nothing in that realm is composed of matter, nothing has a fixed form and, unless the 'otherness' takes on a recognisable form, the experience is incomprehensible. In order to reach me the 'guidance' takes on a form that resonates with my physical and emotional life while my intellect remains somewhat the observer.

Inner space contains no 'choosing between', no value judgement. In that place, forward planning and consequences do not exist, only experiences happen. With each experience comes the possibility of new understanding. I appreciate the help I receive, I love the guides, and my journeys with them have made it possible for me to love my life.

About the Medicine Wheel

When travelling through uncharted territory, it is handy to have a compass and a map. The medicine wheel is a compass and the four directions are the areas of exploration.

Science tells us that carbon is the basic building block of life and that carbon atoms always combine in multiples of four; that makes it a good idea to work, on all levels of expansion, with fours. In this book, I have included diagrams of some of these sets of four as given in the Teachings of Joseph Rael, Beautiful Painted Arrow. I work with them because they aim for highest potential, which is a cogent reason for being in the medicine wheel of Life.

Mystical Teachings are designed to bring insights and inspirations: they are not truths. So for example, where Red is placed in the North, as in this book, any of the other colours could be placed there, but to explore consciousness it is important to work within a frame of reference; in the same way as having a skeleton is important to standing up. A framework that is consistent while being open-ended creates an ideal environment for expanding awareness; that is what I find in Joseph's Teachings. The transformative power is not in the allocation but in the development of the metaphors by the individual mind.

When the Earth was flat, the four directions said it all, but when the Earth became round and was later viewed from space, the metaphor ballooned. A new perception creates a new world of the medicine wheel, which could now be called the medicine sphere, but a change of name is not strictly necessary because a ball bearing is a very efficient wheel.

The ancient form of the medicine wheel, with four directions viewed from the centre, represents the horizontal. The modern form of the wheel adds the vertical, representing the above, the below and the dividing viewing point. That looks like expanding awareness in action, but space on the page has run out!

Other Books by the Author

Tales of Two Coyotes: adventures with power animals

A great deal of fun and some profound suffering are the order of the day (and the night) in this book of 33 shamanic journeys taken while working with various groups of people in seminars led by my Teacher.

There are ten chapters in the book, each one introduced with a colour sketch.

On Trees

Leaving my 'safe' house and walking alone in remote places, I battle with my personal problems. It is a battle that occupies the majority of my attention but while I am engaged upon it, natural forces come in to play with my consciousness.

This book contains colour photos of the places and the birds that feature in the text.

related websites: www.peacechamber.co.uk
www.somethingdoeshappen.co.uk

contact the author: stella@peacechamber.co.uk

images index	page
the Earth	title
carrying	ii
the energy centres	v
a personal colour wheel	6
the Tree above the arbour	18
colours of the four directions	20
more about the directions	31
the centre	31
a sacred knot	35
the oceanic Being	52
en-trance	58
the symbol on the hide	67
the arrow	71
the Black Buffalo	82
Buffalo colour wheel	88
the most ancient Ones	96
Sun Moon Dance Tree	98
distant bells	100
Buffalo spirits	101
Sky, Water, Green	102

Seasons	
Summer Autumn Winter Spring	iv
Summer (white)	1, 8, 61, 86
Autumn (black)	1, 22, 74, 96
Winter (red)	3, 77, 98
Spring (yellow)	7, 40, 85
Winter Solstice (red)	26
New Year (red and yellow)	37
New Beginning (white and black)	103

contents index	page
Summer	1
Dream of a Running Buffalo	
Autumn	1
The Cage	
Winter	3
The Constant Washing Utterly Consumed	
Spring	7
The Strength of the Buffalo	
Summer	8
Sun Moon Dance Killing the Bison Walking with Intent	
Autumn	22
Entering the Cave The Work at Hand	
Winter Solstice	26
The Gift Arrives The Lights The Spirit House of the Buffalo	
A Sacred Knot The Blue Buffalo	
New Year	37
The Long Road The Black Buffalo In the Spirit Lodge	
Spring	40
In the Peace Chamber Through the Spirit Lodge	
The Healing Guide In Deep Water In Deep Earth	
The Silver Streams Dream of Running Buffalo	
Where to Teeter? Moving North	
Summer	61
The Necessity of Falling Calling Supporting the World	
The Exam The Power and I	
Autumn	74
The Consciousness of the Lodge	
Winter	77
Give Up the Drug The Fire Ceremony	
Dark Waters Entering the Black Buffalo	
Spring	85
The Fall	
Summer	86
The Mycelium Draw On the Abundance	
The Silver Cords The Ancient Ones	
Autumn	96
A Song to the Buffalo	
Winter	98
Out Of Darkness Came Light The Abundance of Our Planet	
A New Beginning	103
The Gift of the Green	

www.ingramcontent.com/pod-product-compliance
Lightning Source LLC
Chambersburg PA
CBHW061801070526
44586CB00023B/2669